Eric Lawlor

grew up in Dublin, was educated in the United States and now lives in Texas. He is the author of two previous books, *In Bolivia* and *Looking for Osman: One Man's Travels through the Paradox of Modern Turkey*.

ERIC LAWLOR

Murder on the Verandah

Love and Betrayal in British Malaya

Flamingo
An Imprint of HarperCollins*Publishers*

Flamingo
An Imprint of HarperCollins*Publishers*
77–85 Fulham Palace Road,
Hammersmith, London W6 8JB

Flamingo is a registered trade mark of
HarperCollins Publishers Limited

www.**fire**and**water**.com

Published by Flamingo 2000
9 8 7 6 5 4 3 2 1

First published in Great Britain by
HarperCollins Publishers 1999

ISBN 0 00 655065 7

Set in New Baskerville

Printed and bound in Great Britain by
Clays Ltd, St Ives plc

For Gully

Contents

ACKNOWLEDGEMENTS

It was my great good luck at the beginning of this project to be put in touch with Henry Barlow. Barlow, who lives in Kuala Lumpur and whose family has been associated with the Malay Peninsula for much of this century, has amassed a great wealth of information about British Malaya which, over several months, he was gracious enough to share with me. It was he, too, who introduced me to John Gullick, England's leading Malaya scholar, whose help was not just enormous, but crucial as well. This generous man paid me the great compliment of treating my book as if it were one he was writing himself.

I must thank as well John G. Butcher, whose landmark study *The British in Malaya 1880–1941* I drew on again and again, and who alerted me to the existence of a letter penned by William Steward's brother-in-law in Malaysia's national archives. Tissa Perera, of the Incorporated Society of Planters also provided valuable assistance. His allowing me access to back issues of *The Planter* was especially useful and yielded material that might otherwise have been unavailable to me.

Others helped in significant ways as well: Pennie Redmile in Montreal, Nicola Liddiard in London and Ian Green in Guildford assisted in the search for William and Ethel; Sally Lee found a home for me in Kuala Lumpur; Eloise Rochelle, more computer literate than I, negotiated the Internet on my behalf; Dilys Yap of Badan Warisan Malaysia directed me to the Victoria Institution; Woo Kum Wah conducted me around the Selangor Club; and Terry Barringer, who also has charge of materials in the Royal Commonwealth Society collection at Cambridge University, helped in the choosing of photographs.

To finish, I must extend my gratitude to Gillon Aitken, my remarkable agent: had he not intervened when he did, this book would not exist; and also to the people at HarperCollins: the ever-gracious Annie Robertson, my unflappable editor Rebecca Lloyd and, most especially, Michael Fishwick, the publishing director, whose good humour and patience made writing this book a very happy experience.

List of Illustrations

Unless otherwise stated, all photographs are reproduced by permission of the Syndics of Cambridge University.

'Coelum non animum mutant qui trans mare currunt'
'The sky, but not the heart, they change who speed across the sea'

FROM HORACE, TRANSLATED BY
H. DARNLEY NAYLOR

Preface

On 23 April 1911, Ethel Proudlock, as was her custom on Sundays, attended Evensong at St Mary's Church in Kuala Lumpur. She was well known at St Mary's. From time to time she helped with jumble sales and had recently joined the choir. After the service, a friend invited Ethel to join her for dinner, but she declined. Her husband was going out for the evening, she said; it would give her a chance to write some letters. Then, after checking that the hymnals were in order, she walked home and killed her lover.

Claiming self-defence, she told police that William Steward had turned up unexpectedly that evening and tried to rape her. None of this was true. Steward was there because Mrs Proudlock had invited him, and he died – shot five times at point-blank range – after telling her he was ending their affair.

The Proudlock case, the basis of 'The Letter', the most famous of Somerset Maugham's short stories, galvanized British Malaya. Some Britons insisted she was innocent, but the evidence against her was overwhelming and, after a trial lasting nearly a week, Ethel Proudlock was convicted of first-degree murder and sentenced to die. Preparations to hang her were well advanced when the Sultan of Selangor intervened. Citing her youth and the fact that she was a mother, he granted her a pardon. But the trial had unhinged her. Ordered to leave Malaya, Mrs Proudlock, with her husband and three-year-old daughter, returned to England a virtual invalid.

Until she was arrested, there was little to distinguish Ethel Proudlock from other members of the British community. Like them she was middle-class, seemed perfectly conventional and, to all appearances, was happily married. Ethel Proudlock fitted in, her defenders said. She couldn't possibly be a killer; she was one of them. But the fact remained: Ethel Proudlock *had* killed. Why?

Some suggested that she might be mad. Mrs Proudlock was dangerously unstable, they said; a person whose violent mood-swings had long been the subject of gossip. Others blamed vindictiveness. Ethel made a bad enemy, according to this view. Offend her even slightly, and she was implacable. A third group – this one made up of Kuala Lumpur's Chinese and Malays – attributed the killing to arrogance. Ethel was a member of Malay's ruling caste and, as such, thought she could do as she pleased. When she pulled the trigger that night, she was exercising the prerogatives she believed were hers by virtue of her station.

There is a fourth, more plausible, possibility. When Ethel married, she was a girl of just nineteen whose sheltered background can hardly have prepared her for the pressures and artificialities of colonial life. Might it be the case that those pressures proved too much for her? Answering that question necessarily raises others. What were the British in Malaya really like? How did they comport themselves? Did they enjoy the country? What did they see as their role there? Were they, as some have claimed, a force for good? Or were they opportunists?

Colonial Malaya, often described as 'Cheltenham on the equator', has not lacked for study. Its politics have come in for much attention, as have its economics, but about the British themselves we know surprisingly little. The oversight is regrettable. While the society they created was neither as complex as India's or nearly as grand, it was no less intriguing. No one clung more tenaciously to their ancestral ways than did the British in Malaya; and no one was more convinced of their natural superiority. The institutions they created in that country may well have been unique.

Complicating any effort to take the measure of these people is a controversy set in motion some seventy years ago by Somerset Maugham. Maugham is as much associated with Malaya as Kipling is with the British Raj but, unlike Kipling, who was born in India and spent much of his life there, Maugham visited Malaya only twice: for six months in 1921 and a further four in 1925–26. Yet out of that short acquaintance came his most enduring achievement – a group of short stories bringing Malaya so vividly to life that people named it Maugham Country.

Maugham's portrait of Malaya's colonials is less than flattering. The planters and officials in his stories are dull and mediocre, 'eaten up with envy of one another and devoured by spite'. Their wives are even worse: 'The women, poor things, were obsessed by petty rivalries. They made a circle that was more provincial than any in the smallest town in England . . . They were sheep.'

Cyril Connolly said of Maugham that he had done something never before achieved: 'He tells us exactly what the British in the Far East are like.' The British in Malaya did not agree. They said they'd been betrayed. They had taken Maugham into their homes, introduced him to their friends, made him a guest at their clubs. And for this, he had defamed them. Who are we to believe? This book is an attempt to answer that question.

One thing can be said at the outset: the British changed when they went overseas – a change that was commented on again and again. As one visitor put it: 'Two Englishmen, one here and one at home, might easily be men of different race, language, and religion so different is their outlook and behaviour.'

In so far as it is useful, I have tried to let these people speak for themselves. This is their story after all and it seems only right that I let them help me tell it. I also draw much on the *Malay Mail*. With few sources at my disposal, the *Mail* proved a godsend. Kuala Lumpur's only daily newspaper during this period, it is remarkable not just for the quality of its writing, but also for its knowledge of those whom it was writing about. Recruited in England, the *Mail*'s editorial staff did not simply cover the British community, they formed part of it. They belonged to the same clubs, worshipped at the same church, played on the same rugby teams, shared the same beliefs. At a time when the British in KL (as Kuala Lumpur was colloquially known) numbered between seven and eight hundred, the people these journalists wrote about were, in many cases, known to them personally. I owe the *Mail* a debt of gratitude. Without it, my job would have been very difficult.

Before I begin, a little history. Britain, in the shape of the East India Company, acquired Penang in 1786, Malacca in 1795, and Singapore in 1819. Seven years later, the three territories were amalgamated for administrative purposes. Now called the Straits Settlements, they were ruled from India until 1867 when Penang, Malacca and Singapore became a crown colony and found themselves the responsibility of the Colonial Office.

Now the rest of Malaya beckoned. Uncharacteristically, Britain hesitated – but not out of any high-mindedness. Its reasons were practical: Westminster did not care to become embroiled in Malaya's Byzantine politics. Besides, as long as London controlled the Straits of Malacca – crucial if it were to protect India and safeguard its trade with China – it had little need of Malaya. For years, investors in the Straits Settlements had complained to Britain that it was failing to protect their interests. They had invested large sums of money in Malaya's tin mines, they said – money that the interminable political squabbling in that country now placed at risk. Britain ignored them.

Then the money men changed tack. If Britain would not protect them, London was warned, they would find a country that would. (Germany and Russia were mentioned as likely possibilities.) London was all ears now. The last thing it wanted was a rival in a part of the world it considered its own. And so, in 1874, the government reversed its policy, making protectorates of Perak, Selangor, Sungei Ujong (part of Negri Sembilan) and Pahang, four territories that became the Federated Malay States (FMS) in 1896. Thirteen years later, Britain extended its rule again, this time to embrace the four northern states of Kelantan, Trengganu, Kedah and Perlis, long controlled by Siam. When the lone hold-out – Johore – submitted to British rule in 1914, Britain controlled the Malay peninsula as far north as the Siamese border, an area measuring 70,000 square miles. (The five newcomers declined to join the FMS and were known collectively as the Unfederated Malay States.)

In Malaya, the British employed a formula known as indirect rule, recruiting pliant elites – in this case the sultans – who became, in effect, front-men for colonial rule. The fiction put about was that the sultans, Malaya's traditional rulers, enjoyed considerable discretion, turning to the British only when they needed help. Each state had a Resident – a senior civil servant – who was said to 'advise' the sultan. But no one was in any doubt as to what would happen if that advice were ever disregarded. Essentially, the sultans had a choice: they could do as they were told or be replaced by someone who would.

Because the country was never formally annexed, the British in Malaya convinced themselves that their rule owed nothing to force. This was far from being the case. True, force was rarely used, but no one in Malaya ever doubted it remained an option. When, in 1875, Malays assassinated the first Resident of Perak, the British mounted a punitive expedition that left scores of people dead.

Finally, a few words of explanation. During the period 1900 to 1910, my primary focus in this book, there were three ethnic groups in Malaya: Malays, Chinese and Indians. When referring to all three, I use the term 'Asians'. The term 'Malaya' needs explaining as well. When Mrs Proudlock went on trial in 1911, Malaya comprised the Federated States, the Unfederated States and the Straits Settlements. As a single political entity, Malaya did not as yet exist. The term is convenient, however, and, as others have done, I use it here to mean that part of the Malay peninsula under British rule.

The dollar I mention from time to time is the Straits dollar which, during this period, was worth slightly less than half a crown.

I

Trials

1

'Blood, blood. I've shot a man'

When she returned to her bungalow that Sunday evening, Mrs Proudlock changed from the pink dress with black spots she had worn to church to a pale-green, sleeveless tea gown with a revealing neckline. An odd choice, perhaps, for an evening of letter-writing. She chose the garment, she said later, not because it showed her to good effect, but because it was pleasantly cool. Thus arrayed, she checked to see that her daughter was sleeping (she was), fetched a blotter and an ink-stand and set to work on her correspondence.

She and her husband, William, had moved into this bungalow the previous January. Surrounded on three sides by the Klang river, it stood in the grounds of the Victoria Institution (VI), Kuala Lumpur's premier school. Normally, B. E. Shaw, VI's headmaster, lived here but, four months earlier, Shaw and his family had gone to England on leave. In his absence, Proudlock had been named acting headmaster, which entitled him to use Shaw's house until the latter returned in October.

It was an attractive bungalow. Though it no longer exists – it was demolished when the Klang river, prone to flooding, was rerouted in the late 1920s – Richard Sidney, who succeeded Shaw in 1922, described it in *British Malaya Today* as made of wood and mounted on brick piles 'which get higher as the ground slopes towards the river – ordinarily some 30 yards distant'. The house had its own tennis court and was fairly large, he went on. It 'has rooms bounded by wide verandahs'. The verandah on which Mrs Proudlock wrote her letters that evening contained several of her potted plants, but most of the other furnishings belonged to Mrs Shaw: a rectangular table and some chairs arranged on a square of carpet; a long bookshelf below which was a teapoy; and a large rattan chair bearing some of Ethel's cushions. Light was provided by a single bulb suspended from the ceiling.

The bungalow faced High Street, normally one of Kuala Lumpur's busiest, but this being a Sunday, it was quiet. What sounds there were were muffled by rain. It had been drizzling much of the day and now, as darkness fell, there was a cloudburst, the rain falling so hard that it obscured the 5-foot-high perimeter hedge that divided the school grounds from the street.

Mrs Proudlock was halfway through her second letter when a rickshaw bearing Steward drew up. Less than half an hour later, he was dead. According to Mrs Proudlock's version of events, she was not expecting visitors that evening and had been startled by his arrival. Assuming that Steward had come to see her husband, she informed him that Will was having dinner with a colleague who lived on Brickfields Road, a mile and a half away. If Steward wished, she said, he could see him there. When Steward showed himself reluctant to leave, she suggested he sit down. They made small-talk, she said, discussing the rain and its impact on the rising river. For something to say, Mrs Proudlock mentioned religion, asking Steward if he had been to church that evening. He explained that he attended church very rarely. 'Then you're like my husband,' she said, smiling. 'I'll show you a book he's reading.' She walked to the bookshelf and took down a copy of Leslie Stephen's *An Agnostic's Apology*. She was handing it to Steward when he tried to kiss her. She pushed him away. 'What are you doing?' she said. 'Are you mad?'

Steward answered by grabbing her right wrist and, with his left hand, turned off the light. Frightened now, she tried to break free – and couldn't. When Steward began to raise her dress, she seized his hand and wrenched it away. 'He pulled me towards him,' Mrs Proudlock said. 'He had one arm around my waist and the other on my left shoulder.'

Steward now tried to force her against the wall and, afraid that she might fall, Mrs Proudlock reached out to steady herself. That is when her hand came in contact with a revolver, belonging to her husband, lying on the table.

'I think I must have fired twice then,' she said. Terror had made her mind go blank, she explained, and she couldn't be more precise. 'The next thing I remember I was stumbling. I think it was on the steps [of the verandah], but I'm not sure.'

The shots, striking Steward in the neck and chest, were heard by the rickshaw puller whom Steward had told to wait on High Street. Thinking that help might be needed, the puller was approaching the house, he later told the police, when the door burst open and Steward stumbled down the steps and lurched in his direction. Steward was clutching his chest. Fearing for his own life, the puller fled and had made it as far as the street when three more shots rang out. Glancing back, he saw Ethel Proudlock, gun in hand and still wearing her pale-green tea-gown, standing over Steward's body.

Mrs Proudlock, who claimed to be in a state of shock, said she did not recall following Steward out of the house, nor did she recall shooting him three times in the head while he lay, clinging to life, on the rain-soaked ground. She said it was several minutes before she came to her senses. That was when she called to her cook, who was resting in his room, and ordered him to fetch her husband.

When Proudlock, accompanied by Goodman Ambler, a teaching colleague and the man with whom he had just had dinner, arrived fifteen minutes later, his wife staggered towards him, moaning: 'Blood, blood. I've shot a man.'

'Whom?' he demanded.

'Mr Steward,' she said.

'Where is he?'

'He ran, he ran.'

Mrs Proudlock, her husband would later testify, was incoherent, her dress bore bloodstains, and her hair was in disarray.

When the police arrived, they found Steward, wearing a white suit, brown boots and a mackintosh, lying on his face in a pool of blood. The body was still warm, the *Malay Mail* reported next day, 'and the frightful injuries were a testimony to the terrible execution of the Webley revolver . . . lying some distance away'. According to one police official, there was fresh blood on the Webley's barrel, and Steward's watch was still ticking.

The body was removed to the European Hospital in an ambulance cart. Horse-drawn and equipped with rubber tyres – in 1911, still something of a novelty – the cart would have been a tight squeeze for Steward. Just a few months earlier, the *Mail* had denounced it as absurdly inadequate. It was so short, the paper said, that to accommodate taller patients the back door had to be left open. As if being murdered was not enough, Steward suffered the added indignity of travelling to hospital with his feet protruding.

* * *

Next day the *Mail* reported that the decapitated body of a Tamil had been found near the Convent of the Holy Infant Jesus and that a Chinese man had drowned himself after stabbing his wife. The paper's English readers were unlikely to have paid either item much attention. The talking point that Monday, as it would be for weeks to come, was the story on page 5. Under the headline 'Kuala Lumpur Tragedy; Former Mine Manager Shot Dead; A Distressing Story', it began: 'We regret to record a tragedy which created a profound sensation in Kuala Lumpur when the news became generally known this morning.'

Also that Monday, Mrs Proudlock, accompanied by her husband and still thought to be a woman who had killed to protect her honour, made a court appearance lasting all of three minutes. No evidence was presented, the court expressing the wish that she be spared as much embarrassment as possible. The proceedings ended with her being formally charged with causing William Steward's death – a legal necessity since she herself admitted to killing him. Despite the gravity of the charge, the court took the unusual step of refusing to remand her in custody – no doubt also to spare her feelings – and Mrs Proudlock was released on the payment of two sureties to the amount of $1,000 provided by her father, Robert Charter. A further hearing was fixed for 1st May.

Steward's funeral at 5.30 that Monday afternoon was a forlorn affair. An obituary in the *Mail* lauded him as an energetic miner and, more important in British eyes, an enthusiastic rugby player. But neither his energy nor his enthusiasm seem to have gained him much. A mere fifteen people attended his burial in the Venning Road cemetery, a short distance from Kuala Lumpur's new railway station.

Until a year or two earlier, much ceremony had attended the burial of Britons. At the European Hospital, the coffin was placed on a hand bier and, under escort, was drawn to the cemetery by a detail of splendid-looking Sikh policemen. But in 1909, the police department, for reasons of economy, had ended the practice. Now the bier was drawn by the cemetery's Javanese gardeners. A bit of a come-down, this; and not everyone was pleased. 'In common with many other people,' the *Mail* complained, 'we feel the time has come when it should no longer be necessary to call upon Javanese gardeners or anyone else of an alien race or creed to draw the body of a deceased European along public roads to its last resting place.'

Steward's funeral service was performed by the Revd P. Grahame, a man new to Kuala Lumpur and new as well to presiding over the burials of murder victims. One can imagine his difficulty when recording the event that night in St Mary's register. Under the heading 'Cause of Death', Grahame settled finally for the words 'bullet wounds'. Surrounded as they are by a long list of deaths due to more conventional causes – malaria, dysentery, convulsions and beri-beri – the words when I saw them in 1996 made my blood run cold.

Steward was a shy man and, beyond turning out for a rugby match once in a while, socialized little. He visited the Selangor Club from time to time and, while there, would sometimes share a drink with William Proudlock. He liked Proudlock as much as he had liked anyone, but for all that, he did not have many friends. In 1911, men in Kuala Lumpur spent a lot of time in one another's company, partly because there were not many British women, and partly because, most having been to public schools, they enjoyed other men. Steward seems to have been different. For one thing, most of these men drank a lot; Steward was fairly abstentious. For another, in company, he was ill-at-ease. The bluster and heartiness in the Selangor Club's Long Bar would not have been to his taste. Once in a while, Proudlock prevailed upon him to attend one of his musical 'at homes' but, as hard as he tried, he never succeeded in getting Steward to sing. While the others belted out 'The Road to Mandalay', Steward would sit silently and stare at his shoes.

No one seemed to know much about Steward. He was understood to have been living with a Chinese woman – true, it turned out; he was believed to be forty years old – false: he was closer to thirty-four; and he was thought to have come from somewhere in the British Midlands. In fact, he came from Whitehaven in Cumberland, where he had a mother and a sister with whom he corresponded several times a month. He also helped to support them and regularly sent them money – an income on which they had come to depend and would now greatly miss.

Instead of socializing, Steward seems to have immersed himself in his work. He was respected both as a mining engineer and as someone who did not call attention to himself. This makes his death especially ironic. A person who avoided the public gaze, he would have found the attention hugely embarrassing.

Salak South, the mine he ran until late 1910, prospered under his management. For the month of April that year, the mine produced 122 pikuls of dry ore, an excellent result for a place of its size. (A pikul is the equivalent of $133\frac{1}{3}$ pounds.) The machinery – it was Steward's job to keep it running – worked 594 hours and 35 minutes that month: virtually round the clock.

Kuala Lumpur was a small place then, and Salak South, though just five miles from the Proudlock bungalow, was considered remote. It received few visitors, in part because it was hard to reach and also because it was said to be unlucky. George Cumming, an early backer, invested a fortune in Salak

South and lost every penny. People said the place was cursed, and there must have been times when Steward thought so, too. In 1909, production came to a standstill when the Klang river overflowed, flooding the mine and destroying a lot of expensive equipment. Then, just six months before his own death, one of his colleagues died. It happened quite without warning. 'Mr D. Issacson returned to his bungalow at Salak South about 4 in the afternoon', the *Mail* reported, 'and sat down in a chair from which he never rose, death taking place about 5.30.' The apparently healthy Issacson had suffered a heart attack. Salak South also claimed the lives of numerous labourers. Equipment was primitive. Methods were rudimentary. The great danger, at this mine as at many others, was cave-ins. They could happen in a moment, burying workers who, all too often, died of asphyxiation before frantic colleagues could dig them out.

When Steward and Proudlock chatted in the Selangor Club in December 1910 – the last time they would talk – the miner was looking for work. 'The mine has gone phut,' he said, meaning that the ore had run out. 'I think I have got another post, but I am not sure yet.' In January it was confirmed. Steward was now in the employ of F. W. Barker and Co., a firm of consulting engineers based in Singapore. Though he retained his house not far from the mine, Steward now took to the road, trouble-shooting for some of the largest mines and rubber estates in Selangor. It was a relief to be out of Salak South, he said. All that talk of a jinx had begun to prey on him.

Steward was a man who feared complications. He was methodical and thorough, a man who believed in keeping the record straight. Where details were concerned, he was almost fastidious. In October 1910, he wrote to the *Mail* alerting it to an error it had made: 'In your issue of 28th inst., you publish the managing director's report of the Sungei Raia tin mines and mention that the ground ran 15 catties per yard. Surely this is a mistake and probably should read 1.5 catties per yard. I merely point this out in defence of the management there as they might not see your paper. Yours, etc. W. Steward.' It was a small matter, but none the less revealing, for this was a man to whom small things were important.

Aside from that letter, the *Mail* mentions him only rarely. Steward did not attend the annual ball to mark the King's birthday, and he was never a guest at fashionable weddings, regarding such events as frivolous. He played rugby when work permitted – as much for the exercise as for any enjoyment, one suspects – and, once in a while, got in some tennis. In 1909, he entered a tennis tournament the Selangor Club had organized, but was knocked out in the first round. Rugby was another matter. Steward made a fierce opponent. Malaya had numerous rugby teams and, at one time or another, he seems to have played for most of them. His play was unrelenting, shaped, no doubt, by the great football games of Cumberland legend. Hugh Walpole described one in *Rogue Herries* (1930): 'The goals were distant nearly half a mile the one from the other. There were few rules, if any; all cunning and trickery were at advantage, but brute force was the greatest power of all. There were fifty players a side to start with, although before the game ended there was nearly a hundred a side . . . So that now there was a grand and noble sight, this central mass of heaving men, detached groups of fighters, and the spectators shouting, roaring, the dogs barking as though they were mad.'

A picture of Steward shows him standing on a flight of steps leading to a house – his own, perhaps, in Salak South – and looking a little discomfited. Perhaps the camera has unnerved him. A tall, big-framed man, he is bald and wearing a collar and tie. William Steward, it would appear, liked formality. His right hand rests on his right hip – an attitude that in anyone else would suggest nonchalance but which here makes him look awkward. Knowing how shy he was, it is surprising that he posed for a picture at all, unless he intended to send it to his mother. He'd have done anything for her, even if it meant embarrassing himself.

He was serious, even grave, and threw himself into his work. Perhaps he saw it as redemptive. While it is impossible to say why he came to Malaya – whether to advance the country's interests or his own – he was none the less a caring man, a man who provided for his widowed mother, a man aware of the duty he bore to others.

2

To Hang by the Neck Till She Be Dead

The British in Malaya were still in a state of shock when Mrs Proudlock, still enjoying her freedom, appeared at a magistrate's inquiry on 1st May. 'The painful sensation which the [shooting] occasioned from one end of the country to the other has hardly diminished since the discovery of Mr Steward's body,' the *Mail* reported. By then, opinion had begun to change, many taking the view that Ethel was almost certainly guilty. When, looking considerably younger than her twenty-three years, this 'pretty, blonde-haired woman' took her place at the bar, the room fell silent. One of their own – and female at that – standing in the dock! It proved too much for the magistrate who, his chivalry fired, sent for a chair and told the defendant that she might, if she wished, seat herself near the bench.

He was not the only one in court that day concerned for her comfort. Her lawyer, E. A. S. Wagner, also had her sensitivities in mind when he complained that most of those in the public gallery were Malays and Chinese – what the *Mail* called 'the native element'.

'There are a lot of persons in the court who have no business here,' Wagner said, 'and I think this would tend to affect the prisoner.'

As a person who knew the law, Wagner surely would have known that seeing justice done was everyone's business. Clearly, the presence of non-Europeans made him uncomfortable for another reason: the realization that the trial of Ethel Proudlock had the potential to compromise British prestige. (Wagner was, incidentally, a curious choice to defend Mrs Proudlock. An able lawyer, he and Steward were friends, having often played rugby together. He also seems to have known that his client was guilty. When Somerset Maugham visited Malaya in 1921, it was Wagner who told him of the Proudlock case, even suggesting he write a story about it.)

The police wanted the public excluded, too, but for a different reason. The case involved 'a certain amount of indecency', the magistrate was told. The court was being warned that the evidence to be presented was likely to prove embarrassing, not just to Mrs Proudlock, but to the British generally, and the fewer ears it reached the better for all concerned.

Mr Hereford, the lawyer representing the police, opened the proceedings by summarizing 'the facts in so far as we have been able to ascertain them'. On the night of 23 April, William Steward, he told the court, was dining with two friends in the Empire Hotel when, hearing the clock in the Secretariat building strike nine, he rose suddenly and asked to be excused. He had, he said, an appointment. Then, leaving the hotel in some haste, he flagged down a rickshaw and went directly to the home of the accused.

Besides Mrs Proudlock, the only person in the house when he got there was a cook. Her husband had gone out to dine, and both the *ayah* (nanny) and the 'boy' had the evening off. The cook said he was smoking opium in his room when he heard a man shout, 'Hey! Hey!' This was followed by gunshots, but he took little notice until he heard Mrs Proudlock, from somewhere in the garden and sounding much distressed, telling him to fetch her husband.

When Mr Proudlock returned, he found his wife 'in a very agitated state' and speaking in 'a most unintelligible manner'. She told him that Steward had molested her and made improper proposals. There was gunpowder on her right hand, Hereford continued. 'There is no question that it was she who shot the deceased.'

Hereford then challenged Ethel's claim that Steward's visit was unexpected: 'The deceased stated that he had an appointment. This showed that he must have been aware that he would find the accused in the house by herself . . . It is difficult to see how he could have known this unless the accused had told him. At some point, there was some communication between them.'

He also challenged her claim that Steward had tried to rape her. When the police found Steward, he was fully dressed, and his trousers – what the *Mail* called 'his nether garments' – were buttoned. 'The medical evidence did not show any accomplishment of violation.' Nor was there evidence of a struggle. A teapoy had been overturned but, aside from that, nothing else had been disturbed.

'This,' he added ominously, 'makes her story not very easy to believe.'

Continuing his attack on Mrs Proudlock's probity, Hereford now turned to the matter of her attire. Though she was dining by herself, the accused wore an evening dress which, he had been told, 'is cut very low'. According to her husband, Mrs Proudlock always dressed like this in the evenings, even when she dined alone. But Hereford was sceptical. Allowing that this was not beyond the realm of possibility, it was, he said, 'a question which has to be considered as to whether it does not point to the expectation of a visit from the deceased'.

The evidence had begun to look damning and when the court rose that day, the magistrate, no longer feeling chivalrous, refused to grant an application for bail. For the first time since the shooting, Mrs Proudlock was deprived of her liberty and removed to Pudu gaol, a mile from the courtroom. But old habits die hard. To spare her the indignity of riding to prison in a police van, Detective-Inspector Wyatt drove her there himself in his private car.

It must have been an uncomfortable drive for both of them. What could they possibly have found to say to one another? Wyatt, in charge of the police investigation, could hardly have offered his sympathy. Like many in KL, he did not doubt she was a killer, but there were other obligations on him – obligations of gallantry and the respect due to one's own. A solidarity existed between them – and would do so until such time as the court found her guilty.

Pudu gaol would be Mrs Proudlock's home for the next two-and-a-half months. The prison, completed just six years earlier, covered an area of 7 acres and could accommodate as many as 600 prisoners. Separate from the main building was the female wing which comprised six cells, each containing a plank bed and a wooden pillow. When not locked up, women prisoners were allowed to congregate in a common room where they could knit or even do a little sewing. For their refreshment, the prison provided a pail of weak tea.

In September 1909, the *Mail* had run a long story about Pudu gaol, a story that Mrs Proudlock is almost certain to have read. As well as a daily rice ration, the *Mail* reported, each prisoner received meat or eggs and two kinds of vegetables. Meals were served twice a day – one at 10.15; the other at 4 – and porridge was provided in the early morning. Meals were taken in two large, open-sided sheds to the right of the prison proper. 'All is scrupulously clean and neat,' the story went on. 'There is not a speck of dirt anywhere . . . In the cooking area, there is a marked absence of the somewhat unsavory smells which so often hover over Oriental culinary preparations.'

The regime as reported does not sound especially harsh but, that said, Mrs Proudlock cannot have found it very pleasant. Separated from her husband and her young daughter, she was alone, incarcerated, and facing an uncertain future. As she contemplated that plank bed and wooden pillow, one can imagine her terror.

On the stand the next day, William Proudlock told the court that, on 23 April, he and his wife took a nap after lunch, rose at 4, had tea on the verandah and then put in some target practice, using a revolver she had given him just five days earlier as a birthday present. At 5.25, he had handed the gun to Ethel and told her to put it 'in a safe place'. Both of them then left for church, after which they briefly visited the Selangor Club and went home, where he changed clothes and left for his dinner appointment.

Asked if he and his wife were on good terms, Proudlock said, 'Oh, yes.'

Had he ever had occasion to complain about her moral conduct?

'No,' he said.

What about her conduct in respect to other men: did he ever have cause to complain about that?

'Never.'

Asked why his wife had given him a gun for his birthday, he said that their home in Brickfields Road – the one now occupied by Goodman Ambler – had been broken into the previous August, and they had talked several times since about buying a revolver.

On the day before the shooting, he said, his wife had run into Steward at the Selangor Club and had been forced to talk to him when, passing his chair, he had looked up at her and said hello. In the course of a short conversation, his wife had remarked on how long it was since Steward had been to see them and mentioned that she and her husband had moved to another house. When Steward asked where, she felt she had no choice but to tell him.

Proudlock said he had known Steward for almost two years and considered him a friend. 'He's always behaved as a gentleman towards my wife.'

Summoned home the night Steward died, he found his wife 'in a state of disorder'. Her face was very white, and she was sobbing violently. 'I saw at once that there had been a struggle of some description.' The next day, he saw bruises on her shoulders and on her legs. (The prosecution claimed that these were self-inflicted. A doctor who examined Ethel on Sunday night had found no bruising at all.)

Goodman Ambler, described by Proudlock as 'a great personal friend', then took the stand, testifying that after dinner that Sunday evening he and Proudlock chatted and smoked, and then Will had played the piano, only stopping when the cook arrived.

Mrs Proudlock, when Ambler saw her, looked 'very wild and excited'. Trembling violently, she then became hysterical and almost collapsed. Ambler remembered noticing that her dress was torn below the knee and near the waist. He and Proudlock helped her into the house where Ambler wrapped her in a shawl and her husband gave her a glass of sherry. Lying on a settee, 'she kept half-rising and looking about her very wildly'. When Ambler tried to soothe her, she became angry and told him to shut up. Proudlock took his wife's hand and said, 'Tell us about it, Kiddie.'

As Mrs Proudlock described it, Ambler said, Steward got up when she went to get the book and kissed her saying, 'You're a lovely girl. I love you.'

'She sternly remonstrated with him,' Ambler continued, 'and then shouted for the servants.'

Mrs Proudlock told him that after shooting Steward once, she then shot again. Steward ran from the verandah, and she followed. She remembered stumbling on the steps. And then her mind went blank. When she recovered herself, she was back in the house.

Steward, she said, had lifted her dress and 'tried to spoil me'.

Asked to characterize Mrs Proudlock, Ambler described her as a quiet woman who took pride in her home. 'She and her husband never quarrelled.'

Tan Ng Tee, the rickshaw puller, said he saw Mrs Proudlock – the 'mem' – follow Steward down the steps and stand over his prone body: 'The man made a noise, ''Ah.'' Then he was quiet.'

Tan asked Ethel what had happened to Steward. 'I asked twice,' he said. 'I got no answer. I ran away fast. When I neared the gate, I heard shots: pok, pok, pok. I was frightened. I kept on running.'

Near the body, the police discovered prints which later were found to match Mrs Proudlock's shoes: black pumps with raised heels and two large buckles.

James McEwen, a friend of Steward's, testified to seeing him in the Selangor Club that Sunday. He also saw the Proudlocks. He described Mrs Proudlock as wearing a black 'picture' hat. Asked if he had seen Steward and Mrs Proudlock exchange signals, McEwen said that he had not.

On Day 3 of the proceedings, Will Proudlock asked to take the stand again. He wished, he said, to amend his earlier statement that his wife wore an evening gown when she dined alone. He had meant to say that she wore an evening gown when the *two* of them – he and she – dined alone. It was a clarification that did nothing to help Ethel's case; if anything, it reinforced suspicions that she had donned this garment only because she expected company.

In the event it hardly mattered. Dismissing Ethel's claim that she had acted in self-defence, the magistrate closed the inquiry by reading the charge against her: 'That on or about April 23, 1911, in Kuala Lumpur in Selangor, you did commit murder by causing the death by shooting of one William Crozier Steward and thereby committed an offence punishable under section 302 of the penal code.' She was ordered to stand trial at the next assizes.

Mrs Proudlock cried and trembled as the charge was read, and it was some time before she could compose herself. Then, with some difficulty, she struggled from the dock and, her face stained with tears, left the court on her husband's arm.

Mrs Proudlock would languish in Pudu gaol for almost six weeks before Kuala Lumpur next saw her. On 11 June she appeared in the Supreme Court where her trial opened before Mr Justice Sercombe Smith. Ethel was dressed in white and wore a hat whose veil concealed much of her face. According to the *Mail*, 'she looked very pale as she took her place in the dock'. The public gallery was almost empty.

It is a little ironic that Mrs Proudlock, an aspiring thespian, had recently appeared to good reviews in an amateur production of Gilbert and Sullivan's *Trial by Jury*, but would now enjoy no such privilege herself. Jury trials had been abolished in Malaya some years earlier, in large part because the pool of jurors, being confined to Britons – the only group thought capable of reaching judicious decisions – was necessarily small.

Another reason for abolition had to do with a distrust of lawyers, most of whom were considered cynical and tendentious and all too likely to play on jurors' emotions. Instead of trial by jury, Malaya employed the assessor system – later a source of much controversy. Under this arrangement, the defendant faced a triumvirate comprising a judge and two assistants. The judge interpreted the law, and the assistants, members of the public who in most cases had no legal training at all, *assessed* the evidence 'in the cold light of reason'. And then all three voted, verdicts being determined by a simple majority.

During the six weeks since Ethel had last been seen in public, rumours had been circulating that she and Steward were lovers. This was mere conjecture, Sercombe Smith reminded his assessors that first morning. Steward had attended the musical 'at homes' Will Proudlock liked to organize and, like many others, sometimes ran into the Proudlocks at the Selangor Club. This in no way proved, he said, that Steward and Mrs Proudlock had been intimately involved.

Mrs Proudlock, Sercombe Smith went on, said she killed Steward in self-defence: 'I was protecting my person as I am entitled to do.' But had Steward really tried to rape her? That, too, had still to be proved, and the assessors' decision in the matter would determine the case's outcome.

The first to take the stand was the defendant's husband who told the court that his marriage was a happy one. Ethel 'was always very attentive and affectionate'. She had been nineteen when he married her in 1907. Her health had been bad, he said, and they left for England within hours of the wedding. On the journey home, she was attended several times by the ship's doctor. Since her return to KL in November 1908, her health had been poor. 'She's always been very nervous and easily frightened.'

G. C. McGregor, one of Ethel's doctors, then described her medical history in some detail – information which the *Mail* chose not to publish for reasons of propriety. (The details that follow were taken from a transcript of the trial sent to the Colonial Office.) Ethel had numerous problems, McGregor said: profuse leucorrhoea (an abnormal vaginal discharge), excessive and irregular menstruation, relaxed genitalia, a collapsed uterus and a tender ovary. There was more: the lips of her vulva were malformed, and her vagina contained large quantities of pus. McGregor had urged her to have an operation, but Mrs Proudlock, as he put it, 'kept putting off the evil day'. Ethel, he finished, was a delicate girl who did not possess the strength of a normal person. When Steward confronted her, she became hysterical and had fired those shots, not to kill him, but to rid herself of an impending calamity.

Dr Edward MacIntyre, an assistant surgeon assigned to KL's General Hospital and the man who examined Mrs Proudlock on the night of the murder, was asked if her eyes looked dazed. 'Dazed' didn't seem the right word, he said; as he remembered them, they looked intelligent. He did not get the impression that the accused had just experienced a severe mental shock.

JUDGE: It has been stated that the accused struggled her hardest. In your opinion was the condition of the accused compatible with her having struggled her hardest?

MACINTYRE: No.

JUDGE: Compatible with any kind of struggle?

MACINTYRE: Yes.

Inspector Farrant, who searched Steward's house in Salak South, said he found clothes belonging to a European female and a European child in Steward's bedroom. It is not known if these belonged to Mrs Proudlock and her young daughter; the prosecution did not pursue the subject. The only letters in the house, Farrant said, were from the dead man's mother and sister in Whitehaven.

While Farrant was searching the house, the court was told, a Chinese woman, presumably Steward's lover, asked the policeman if he knew of Steward's whereabouts. When told that he'd been murdered, she burst into tears. With the exception of members of his family, this woman may have been the only person to weep for Steward, the only person who actually cared about him. In the eyes of Ethel's dwindling supporters, Steward's association with a Chinese woman proved beyond all doubt the extent of his degeneracy. A moral man, a man of any character, didn't do such things. If Steward was capable of sleeping with a Chinese, he was capable of anything. For such a person, raping a white woman was a very small step.

Recalled to the stand, Proudlock had to fight back tears when asked to describe his wife's demeanour after she had retired that evening: 'During the night, I saw her muttering something in what I thought was her sleep. I got out of bed. I put on the lights, and she was on her back with her eyes staring up. I said, "What is it, Kiddie?" She made no reply and turned over.'

'What was the object of her putting on the gown?' the judge wanted to know. 'To look beautiful?'

'No. To be cool.'

There were even fewer people in the public gallery when the case resumed next morning, but after lunch the court was full. The day was unusually hot, and a supporter had provided Mrs Proudlock with a paper fan.

For the trial's fourth day, Mrs Proudlock, who was something of a clothes-horse, wore a white straw hat trimmed with brown ribbon. Whereas earlier she had seemed dazed and had taken little interest in the proceedings, she now chatted with her counsel before the judge arrived and then talked at length with her husband.

First to take the stand was Albert Reginald Mace, who had shared a house with Steward until March 1910.

JUDGE: He was not an immoral person?
MACE: No.
JUDGE: He was quite a moral man?
MACE: Yes.

Mace said he had never seen Steward intoxicated; he was a temperate man. The most he had ever seen him drink was two *stengahs* (whisky and soda) a day.

For the first time since the trial began, Mrs Proudlock now took the stand in her own defence. Speaking in a weak voice, she said she had known Steward for two years, during which time he had dined at her home on many occasions.

A day later, she seemed more in charge of herself, answering questions in a voice that no longer wavered. When she rose to fetch *The Agnostic's Apology*, she told the court, Steward grabbed her and said, 'Never mind the book. You look bonnie. I love you.'

Mrs Proudlock now broke down and, hiding her face in her hands, 'wept bitterly'. She said it had been her intention to fire over Steward's head. (Later she would say she didn't know the gun was loaded.) She had not wanted to hurt Steward; her intention was only to frighten him.

'Do you remember', she was asked by Hastings Rhodes, the public prosecutor, 'standing over the body of Mr Steward some seconds before firing?'

'No.'

'I suggest you fired three shots into Mr Steward's body while he lay on the ground. You must have stood over the body anything from three to ten seconds before making up your mind to fire.'

Mrs Proudlock said she had no memory of standing anywhere. After firing that first shot on the verandah, she became oblivious.

Asked by Rhodes if she had visited Salak South when her husband was in Hong Kong for three weeks in 1909, she said she had not.

'Do you remember spending a night at Salak South and having breakfast there in the morning?'

'No.'

She did admit, however, that during her husband's absence, Steward once visited her. But on that occasion, she said, there were several other people present. And, she added, the evening had been miserable. She denied that she and Steward had spent part of that evening alone together in a car. She said she and her guests had gone for a drive in the Lake Gardens, but she had been in one car and Steward in another.

The suggestion that she and Steward had been lovers seems to have upset Mrs Proudlock far more than the altogether more serious charge that she had killed him. Speaking through her counsel, she told the judge she would much rather be convicted of capital murder than leave the court bearing the taint of adultery.

Sercombe Smith, who during this trial seems to have thought of little but Mrs Proudlock's low-cut gown, now intervened to ask if she were wearing 'any underthing' the night Steward died.

Mrs Proudlock answered that she was wearing a chemise and stockings.

'Was it your custom to do so?'

'Yes, whenever I wore an evening tea gown.'

Then she wasn't wearing drawers?

'It is my habit not to wear drawers when I wear a frock with thick lining.'

On 15 June, Dr McGregor took the stand again and testified that when he examined Mrs Proudlock on 24 April, her expression had been one of restrained terror. When he asked her how she felt, she said, 'This is a horrible incident, and it's not yet finished. It seems as if someone is gripping my brain. If it does not stop, I shall go mad.'

The last person to give evidence was Thomas Cooper, the doctor who performed Steward's post-mortem. He found 'no signs of recent sexual connection', he said; 'there were smegma on Steward's prepuce, but no spermatozoa on the body.' Cooper then undermined his value as a witness by claiming that, to rape a woman, a man would first have to render her unconscious. 'Even though a man may overpower a woman and put her on the ground and be within an inch of accomplishing his purpose, the slightest movements of a woman's buttocks would prevent his purpose being carried out.'

Summing up for the defence, J. G. T. Pooley described the Proudlocks as living 'on the most harmonious terms'. The prosecutor, he said, claimed that Steward's visit had been arranged. But where was the proof? It was possible, he conceded, that when Steward arrived at the bungalow that night, 'some little smile' on Mrs Proudlock's part may have led him to believe 'he was being graciously received'. It was not unknown, he added, for men to make this kind of mistake.

Killing Steward was the least of her intentions, he said. She wished only to be rid of him. An emotional, hysterical woman, she became mad with terror and lost all sense of what she was doing. The person in the dock was but a young girl, he went on. A young girl with a baby face. Did she look like someone who would commit a deliberate, atrocious murder? Of course not. Such a thing was impossible to imagine for the very good reason that she had absolutely no motive. When she fired, she had no idea what she was doing. Steward's attack on her modesty had deprived her of judgement and reason.

'I submit to you, gentlemen,' Pooley went on, 'that in this country where there are few white ladies and many men,' there are times when a woman must act to protect herself. 'And I ask you to say that a man who made such an attack on a virtuous woman is a brute, a beast; nay lower than a beast. He is a snake, and I ask you to say that one should no more hesitate to kill such a noxious animal than one should a snake. I ask you in the name of all that is manly, all that is straightforward, if you believe the deceased did commit that abominable outrage on the accused to say she was justified in brushing it away, crushing and absolutely extinguishing it.'

It was a good speech, though not good enough to convince the judge. At 4.47 on 16 June, Sercombe Smith, having finished reviewing the evidence, turned to his assessors, P. F. Wise and R. C. M. Kindersley.

'Mr Wise,' he asked, his voice barely audible in the packed courtroom, 'have you considered your verdict on the charge of murder?'

Wise answered that he had. 'My verdict says she is guilty.'

The judge now addressed Kindersley. 'Mr Kindersley, have you considered your verdict on the charge of murder?'

KINDERSLEY: My verdict says she is guilty.
JUDGE: I concur.

Sercombe Smith turned to the prisoner and asked if there was any reason why she should not be sentenced to death. According to the *Mail*, Mrs Proudlock had become ashy white in countenance and stared blankly in front of her. With one hand, she gripped the rail of the dock and in the other held a bottle of smelling salts. She did not answer.'

It was now noticed that William Proudlock was not in court, and Robert Charter, Ethel's father, left the room to look for him. When the two returned a minute later, Mr Proudlock, 'in a state of great distress', walked to the edge of the dock.

Addressing Ethel, the judge now proceeded. 'I understand you have nothing to say.'

She nodded her head and then said no.

The court registrar called for silence while the sentence was being passed.

'The court then became very silent,' the *Mail* reported. Donning the black cap and 'speaking in an emotional voice, the judge passed the terrible sentence: "I sentence accused to hang by the neck till she be dead." Accused continued to stare wildly in front of her and seemed unable to realize that her death sentence had been passed. On seeing her husband standing by her, the accused burst into tears. Her husband supported her and, for a few seconds, the court witnessed a painful scene. The husband, leaning over the rail of the dock, kissed his wife several times and spoke consolingly to her. But to no avail. She broke down completely, and her sobs could be heard all over the court. Many remained to witness the pathetic scene.'

In a state of near-collapse, Mrs Proudlock, clinging fast to her husband's arm and supported by several friends, had virtually to be carried from the courtroom. This time, Detective-Inspector Wyatt was not on hand to drive her back to prison. The proprieties had ceased to apply. Ethel Proudlock was a convicted killer.

3

A Profound Sensation

The Proudlock case transfixed Malaya. 'In the history of the FMS,' said a *Mail* editorial, 'the case is without a parallel . . . It is not exaggerating . . . to say that news of the death sentence passed upon the accused woman came as a great shock throughout Selangor and further afield.'

To understand the trial's impact, it is necessary to bear in mind that, in 1911, there were only 700 Britons in Kuala Lumpur and a little over 1,200 in the entire FMS. This was a relatively small group whose members, bound by culture and language and social background, took an obsessive, almost familial interest in one another. No matter how trivial, everything they did was considered news. In the *Mail*, items such as, 'Mr P. C. Russell has taken to a motorbicycle', and 'We regret to learn that Mrs Noel Walker is laid up with rheumatic gout', were daily fare. Banal fare, perhaps, but then British Malaya was a banal place. Nothing much happened there. The British were ever complaining that the country was dull. Ethel Proudlock changed all that. One of their own had been convicted of murder. Not only was the victim English – which introduced an element of fratricide – but the perpetrator was a woman. Ethel Proudlock had violated two taboos – three if you counted her infidelity. The British in Malaya were understandably stunned.

What worried them particularly was the impact this would have on their standing, not just locally as the standard-bearers of civilization, but in England, where many people saw them as sybarites, a charge that deeply offended them. In their own estimation, they were models of rectitude: conscientious, enterprising, industrious – everything one would expect of a group whose job it was to build an empire. At great risk to themselves, they believed, they had come to Malaya to bring civilization to a backward people And did those at Home (in the *Mail*, 'Home' was always capitalized) thank them for it? Quite the contrary; they were defamed and vilified.

Few in England knew anything about Malaya. They were ignorant of the heat, the insects, the monotony, the risks to life and limb. They couldn't even find it on the map. Letters were for ever turning up in the FMS capital addressed to Kuala Lumpur, India; Kuala Lumpur, China; Kuala Lumpur, Tibet; even – and this is my favourite – Kuala Lumpur, Asia Minor. 'This diversity, of course, has its charm,' the *Mail* remarked in 1910, 'but it's not particularly gratifying to those who think that the FMS should, owing to their increasing importance, be brought geographically to an anchor.'

They had been brought to an anchor now. Word of the Proudlock trial quickly spread beyond Malaya. It became a topic of conversation not just in India and Australia, Canada and New Zealand, but in the British capital itself. 'Several London newspapers which arrived . . . last night', the *Mail* reported with some embarrassment, 'publish fairly long reports of the Kuala Lumpur tragedy. One paper devotes nearly a column to the affair under the heading, Sensational

Case in British Colony.' (Another gratuitous offence, this: the Straits Settlements were a colony; the Federated Malay States were a protectorate.) People were finally talking about Malaya, but what they were saying did not redound to its credit.

Small though the British community was, Steward's murder polarized it. Some saw the trial as a travesty and claimed that a gross injustice had been done. A decent woman had defended her honour and, instead of being celebrated for her courage, now found herself under sentence of death. It was unconscionable, these people said, none more passionately than 'Irishman'.

In a letter to the *Mail*, 'Irishman' described Mrs Proudlock as a modest, quiet and unassuming woman, devoted to her husband and her daughter. 'I put it to the community at large,' he wrote, 'is not a woman justified in defending her honour which, to many, is dearer than their lives? Or are we to consider our wives and daughters so little above the brute creation that a defence of their honour is unjustified by the laws of the land we live in.' Having had his say, he felt compelled to explain himself: 'I append the nom de plume Irishman . . . because although we are impulsive and demonstrative as a race, in no country in the world is the honour of women held in higher reverence.'

There were other testimonials. 'Having known Ethel Proudlock intimately for the past 11 years,' 'FMS' wrote, 'I feel it is due her to say that, in all those years, I have found her to be sincere, truthful, modest and chaste in conversation.' Another letter a day later applauded her bravery: 'The death sentence is little likely to prevent the English woman doing her duty in a similar emergency, I trust. Thank God that there are many of them of Mrs Proudlock's pluck.'

Modest? Chaste? Death before dishonour? Even in 1911, there were parts of the world where much of this would have sounded dated. British Malaya, though, was not one of them. Though Victoria had died a decade earlier, Kuala Lumpur was still very much a Victorian enclave. Many of its inhabitants had come to the FMS in the 1890s and, by 1911, the values and attitudes they'd taken with them, instead of withering had, if anything, grown more vigorous. An example of this is the view they took of women.

One of the most popular books in the Kuala Lumpur Book Club – facetiously known as the Dump of Secondhand Books – was John Ruskin's *Sesame and Lilies.* The volume contained what may be Ruskin's most famous lecture, 'Of Queen's Gardens'. The lecture – a key Victorian document and hugely influential – defined the ideal woman as a creature both sweet and passive, obedient and gentle, pliant and self-deprecating. The title refers to Ruskin's view that a home run by a woman conscious of her responsibilities is more than just a dwelling place; it becomes a place of enchantment, a garden graced by a queen.

In 1911 in Malaya, women were still expected to conform to the Ruskin paradigm: a person who didn't seek to realize herself, but was content to be her husband's instrument – his subject, even. Always aware of the duty she bore him, she ministered to his needs and deferred to his better judgement. If called upon to do so, she was ready 'to suffer and be still' – the words Sarah Stickney Ellis used in 1845 to describe a woman's highest duty. But a life of self-renunciation was not enough; she had also to be pure. Purity was a woman's greatest asset. Take it away and she promptly became a brute. It was a woman's job to civilize men, to raise them up. (Here, her task was analogous to that of Malaya's empire-builders.) She had to be 'the angel in the home', a moral touchstone to whom others turned for guidance. It was on this account that the so-called fallen woman inspired such horror. A woman who strayed from the path of virtue didn't just jeopardize her own life, she jeopardized the lives of those who most depended on her: her husband, whose shame now made him the object of scorn; and her offspring, who would ever bear the taint of their mother's sin.

Mrs Proudlock, if she did not own one herself, would certainly have been familiar with a print that hung in many Malayan homes: Augustus Egg's *Past and Present No. 1*. It depicts a man, slumped in a chair and deep in shock, clutching in his left hand a letter apprising him of his wife's adultery. His wife, meanwhile, has collapsed at his feet – the collapse as much moral as physical – while his two small daughters, motherless now and little understanding the tragedy that has overtaken them, innocently build a house of cards.

Concupiscence in a wife was considered monstrous, not least because it threatened the social and moral order. During sex, men liked to believe, a woman gritted her teeth and tried valiantly to think of higher things: her garden, perhaps, or her needlepoint. An adulteress was worse than a whore who, very often, could blame her degradation on poverty. A middle-class woman had no such excuse. She was a person of means, even if, in most cases, those means belonged to her husband.

In British Malaya, as in other parts of the empire, the erring woman was an object of such revulsion that even murder inspired less horror. During the trial, the British were not nearly as concerned that Mrs Proudlock had killed a man as they were that she might have broken her marriage vows. Ethel knew this as well as anyone which is why, speaking through her lawyer, she told the court that as much as her life meant to her, her reputation mattered more. It is also why the *Mail* expressed such satisfaction when Sercombe Smith gave the allegations of adultery short shrift. 'The insinuations made against the moral character of Mrs. Proudlock were very serious,' said the paper, 'and we will be supported by everyone when we express our pleasure at their withdrawal and the manner in which [the judge] laid emphasis on the fact that she was completely cleared of any such imputation.'

While 'Irishman' and others like him continued to proclaim Ethel Proudlock's innocence, while petitions circulated and defence funds were set up, while cables were sent to the British king, and people demanded a return to the jury system, there were those who believed that the condemned woman had got her just desserts.

Rumours abounded. It was whispered that Ethel had been in love with Steward for over a year and had been seen more than once hurrying to his home in Salak South; that she despised her husband and longed to be rid of him; that she and Steward had meant to elope.

It was also claimed that she had had not just one affair, but several – and some of those concurrently. In one of the more sensational versions of what supposedly transpired that night, it wasn't Ethel who killed Steward, but a second suitor who, dropping by on a whim, took it amiss that another was making free with the object of his affections.

The source of this story was an Indian nightwatchman who, minutes after hearing the shots, claimed to have seen a fully-dressed Englishman swim across the Klang river, then in flood and swarming with crocodiles. Since Ethel now had a corpse on her hands, fleeing like that was hardly gallant, but because the killer was a favourite of hers – the story gets more and more outlandish – she sacrificed herself to save him, telling the police it was she who pulled the trigger.

In another version, no less bizarre, William Proudlock was the killer. Having learned that his wife had taken a lover, he set a trap for Steward that Sunday, waiting in the hedge until the miner turned up and then dispatching him. Why, then, did Mrs Proudlock stand trial? Because, this story goes, her husband threatened to expose her: unless she admitted to the crime, he would reveal her to the world as an adulteress.

So many theories. For most, the temptation to speculate was irresistible. Even Mabel Marsh succumbed. According to Marsh, the normally sensible headmistress at KL's Methodist Girls' School, it was William Proudlock who had tired of Ethel, not the other way around, and it was he who wanted a divorce. But how? The lady was above reproach. So Will recruited Steward and a plan was hatched: Steward would go to the bungalow, seduce Ethel, and Will would 'discover' them *in flagrante.* But the fates willed otherwise, and when Will got home, after being delayed by all that rain, Steward was already cold.

In a letter to the *Mail*, one man dismissed these stories as mean-spirited and vicious and accused his countrymen of lacking chivalry. 'How men can attack a defenceless woman in her darkest hour of overwhelming grief is a mystery,' he wrote. 'Surely such conduct is altogether inconsistent with the conduct of a man and that of a gentleman.'

As the controversy grew, even Sercombe Smith came in for criticism. The charges became so virulent in some cases that the *Mail* had to tell its readers to desist. While it sympathized with Mrs Proudlock, the paper said, 'we decline to associate ourselves with the hysterical outbursts which have followed the judicial decision . . . Correspondence has already appeared in our columns touching upon the case, and the opinions of our readers will receive publicity within limits. But for those who have gone to all kinds of adjectival extremes in the attempt to splutter forth their wrath against the judge and assessors, it may be added that their effusions will find the oblivion of the waste-paper basket.'

The attack was now taken up by *Capital*, a paper published

in Calcutta. Describing the trial as 'a powerful and fearful failure of justice', *Capital* said it evoked the worst excesses of Bardell vs. Pickwick. 'The verdict is ridiculous,' it went on. 'If, as the prosecution endeavoured to prove, the man was lured to the house with the intention that he should be shot out of revenge, jealousy or pique, no mercy should be shown. If, on the other hand, the unfortunate woman shot the wretch in defence of her honour, who will dare to say she was wrong? It comes to this: that in the FMS a woman who defends her honour must look for no mercy from a British judge and assessors.'

Sercombe Smith, it said, was a buffoon who had prostituted his office 'and defiled the ermine which British judges are supposed to wear'. *Capital* then proposed some rough justice of its own. It was time to apply lynch law, it suggested. Tar and feather the man. And when that was done, string him up.

All this was profoundly gratifying to the Proudlock camp. The authorities, though, were not amused. When the *Times of Malaya*, a paper published in Ipoh, reprinted the *Capital* article, the government denounced it as defamatory and went to law. The editor of the *Times*, having badly underestimated official sensitivities, now tried to make amends. He issued an apology in which he described the article as 'abominable and scurrilous'. The government was not appeased, however, and, on 31 July, a court ordered the editor to pay a fine of $350.

Horace Bleackley, author of *A Tour in Southern Asia*, now added to the furore by suggesting that assaults like the one Ethel supposedly endured were not uncommon. Malaya, he said, was full of men like Steward, whom he characterized as one of the many satyrs 'infecting' those colonies where men outnumber women. This was considered a low blow, not least because Bleackley made these charges in a letter to London's *Daily Mail*. The community was outraged: one of its own had betrayed it. The *Malay Mail* thought so, too. 'We are not aware', the paper said in an editorial, 'that less respect and consideration are shown for European ladies in communities in Selangor than in an ordinary London suburban community. We may go further than that and say that quite the contrary is the case. We have the idea that nowhere at Home are women more honoured and esteemed than here, and there are no signs that the position held by them for so long is likely to change.'

It did not change. Writing as late as 1932, George Bilainkin, who edited Penang's *Straits Echo*, complained that women were still being treated as if they were royals. 'In the tropics,' he wrote, 'the simplest looking woman keeps every man on his mettle, for the plainest woman is a goddess.' As Bilainkin described it, this made for extravagant behaviour. 'Men are everywhere,' he went on, 'paying them idiotic compliments, running almost to greet them, jumping up as soon as they show signs of rising – spreading a smile as wide as a cat's at a woman's sign of willingness to dance.'

The authorities in Malaya had badly underestimated the impact of the Proudlock case. Could they have known the uproar it would cause and the divisions it would engender, it is unlikely that Ethel would ever have been tried. When the death sentence was handed down, there were complaints that the judge had been over-zealous; that he had failed to understand the intentions of those in power.

Mrs Proudlock had become a major embarrassment. Though she had her enemies, few wished to see her die on the gallows, and so it was decided to seek clemency for her. Just hours after the verdict was read, William Proudlock cabled the Secretary of State for the Colonies in London and appealed for a royal pardon in consideration of George V's approaching coronation.

Others were busy, too. Her lawyers lodged an appeal, claiming that no motive had been established; the prosecution had unfairly painted Mrs Proudlock as a libertine; and it had not been proved that a person suffering a deep mental shock is accountable for her actions.

Also making the rounds were several petitions seeking a reprieve and addressed to the Sultan of Selangor. 'The European petition has been signed by over 200 persons, and the Indian petition by about 500,' the *Mail* reported. 'A petition is also being prepared for signatures among the leading members of the Chinese community.'

A cablegram was dispatched to Her Majesty the Queen in Buckingham Palace. 'We undersigned European women in Kuala Lumpur', it read, 'implore pardon at this coronation time for Ethel Proudlock, aged 23, wife and mother, sentenced to death for shooting.' The cost of the cablegram, the *Mail* reported with some pride, 'was almost $150'.

In Great Shelford, Cambridgeshire, Will Proudlock's seventy-two-year-old father weighed in as well, writing to the Foreign Office to seek the help of Sir Edward Grey. In a letter dated 16 June, this former millwright told Grey that he had once worked on his estate and appealed to him to save 'my poor daughter-in-law from the horrible fate awaiting her'. In poor health now – his sight was failing – Proudlock referred to Steward's death as 'this crushing calamity which has come upon me in my old age'. Ethel had not murdered anyone, he said; all she had done was defend herself 'from being outraged by a brute'. Proudlock told Grey that he had once been a coal miner and had 'started work in the pit as trap-door keeper at the age of eight years'. The letter ended: 'I am, Sir, in dire distress, yours obediently, William Proudlock.'

On 26 June, the younger Proudlock received a reply from the Colonial Office informing him that if he sought leniency for his wife, he had best appeal to the Sultan of Selangor: 'I am directed to inform you that . . . the exercise of the prerogative of mercy is a matter for the discretion of the local government with which His Majesty the King does not desire to interfere.'

Newspapers in England, making much of what they saw as constitutional anomalies, claimed to be shocked that an 'Oriental potentate' would have it in his power to determine Mrs Proudlock's fate. But since even Lord Northcliffe must have known that this, like all the sultan's other powers, was circumscribed, the 'shock' was largely bogus. Besides, this 'potentate' had a good heart. Richard Winstedt, who wrote the first Malay–English dictionary, described him as 'a mild gentleman of refined manners and instincts' whose hobbies 'were religion, cookery and wood-carving'. (According to Winstedt, who was recovering from malaria when Steward died, the nurses looking after him in a Malayan hospital had no sympathy for Ethel. She had disgraced her sex, they said, and, in their estimation, hanging was too good for her. That changed, though, when the verdict was handed down. Then they went around the wards pleading with their patients to press to have her pardoned.)

Also on 26 June, the sultan responded to the petition signed by the European ladies: 'In reference to your petition praying for a free pardon for Mrs. Proudlock now under sentence of death, I am directed to inform you that an appeal has been entered against the verdict and that the consideration of your petition will be deferred until the result of the appeal is declared or the appeal is abandoned.'

To the shock and dismay of her supporters, her legal advisers among them, Mrs Proudlock now withdrew her appeal and announced that she was placing herself entirely at the sultan's mercy. In a letter sent to Wagner but clearly intended for public consumption, she said it would be at least a month before the court of appeal took up her case, and she feared that the wait would prove too much for her.

'The suspense is simply awful,' she wrote. 'I am, as you are probably aware, in a condemned cell. Each day and night the only time I am not locked up behind iron bars is when the jailer takes me out for exercise. The continual supervision has got on my nerves to the extent that I feel that another month of it would deprive me of my reason.

'I have a horror of appearing in court again. My recollections of it are so terrible that I cannot bear the idea of having to go through it all over again. I do not feel that any punishment could cause me more pain and suffering than I have already endured. Conscious of my own innocence of the terrible charge against me, I shrink from being stared at and pointed out as a condemned criminal.

'I am told that various petitions have been sent to His Highness the Sultan asking that I may be pardoned. I hope that he may be made to take pity on my sufferings.'

Conscious that her decision would disappoint her supporters, she extended her apologies: 'I hope they will understand. Perhaps if they saw my cell they would say so. I am unfeignedly grateful to them all, and I will ask my husband to convey to the ladies of Penang and other parts my sincerest thanks for their sympathy to one in such terrible trouble as myself.'

Not everyone was mollified. 'No one could have read the pathetic letter which Mrs. Proudlock addressed to her counsel unmoved,' the *Mail* said on 1 July. 'On the whole, however, we cannot help thinking that it would have been better had the appeal been allowed to proceed.'

The ambivalence was understandable. While her supporters did not wish to see her suffer, an appeal might have resulted in an absolute acquittal. That would now not happen. Even if, as seemed more and more likely, the sultan *did* grant her a pardon, the verdict of murder would stand, and Ethel would remain a convicted killer. Some saw this as less than satisfactory. They wanted all taint of guilt removed because only when she was exonerated would they be exonerated. As things stood now, there would always be a doubt. Had this woman – to all appearances chaste and modest – killed her lover in a fit of jealous rage? And if she had, what did it say about *other* apparently modest women?

Events now began to move swiftly. On 1 July, the *Mail* expressed its pleasure that 'intimation that the sentence will be commuted' had been relayed to Mrs Proudlock and that the good lady had been moved from Death Row and was again in 'one of the ordinary cells of the jail . . . She will know the extent to which the sentence has been commuted in a couple of days – on Monday, we believe, when the Sultan of Selangor is to sit in council to deal with the matter.'

At Monday's council meeting, however, Mrs Proudlock was not mentioned. Just why is hard to say – unless there was dissension. While the sultan had made it clear that he favoured a pardon, many British officials, convinced of Ethel's guilt, pressed instead for a life sentence. They did so for political reasons, arguing that as damaging as the murder had been, setting her free would make a mockery of British claims that, before the law, rulers and ruled alike were treated equally. Five days of intense negotiation followed after which the council met again in Klang, on Saturday, 8 July. Those present included J. O. Anthonisz, the acting British Resident, and Sercombe Smith, who brought along the notes he had taken at the trial.

Sercombe Smith told the council that Ethel's conduct 'points rather to revenge than to human frailty. Her firing was, in my opinion, deliberate and unjustifiable.' The court, he said, had 'utterly disbelieved her evidence'. Granting her a pardon would be a mistake.

The council's British members agreed, but the sultan stood firm, and Anthonisz chose to let him have his way. 'I have little doubt', Anthonisz said later, 'that if the native element had been eliminated and the sultan had not expressed such a strong wish, the result would have been a commutation of the sentence to a term of imprisonment.'

Anthonisz was much criticized for this decision. People said he was weak and, in a matter as grave as this, should have stood his ground. Anthonisz was not much liked. Though educated at Cambridge, he was Ceylonese which, in race-conscious KL, did little to win him friends. But in this case, at least, the charge of weakness was unfair. Anthonisz was one of just a few British officials who considered Ethel innocent. Her evidence sounded rehearsed, he said, 'but I am not prepared to go so far as to say that it was not piled up on a foundation of truth . . . I think it was not unlikely that the motive alleged was the correct one.'

In some quarters, the pardon provoked an uproar. 'There is nothing to support the theory of attempted rape and a good deal that tells against it,' one official said. Sercombe Smith was especially critical and accused the sultan of acting despotically. His action amounted to a slur, he said, which no self-respecting judge should have to endure.

The pardon had come with a condition. In return for being released from prison, Mrs Proudlock would have to leave the country. Though she had no choice in the matter, she was probably glad to go. She must have understood that Malaya had washed its hands of her. It was not a kind place. If she had stayed, her life would have been a hell.

News of the pardon reached KL at three o'clock that Saturday afternoon and, two hours later, Anthonisz signed the papers authorizing Mrs Proudlock's release. At nine that evening, the *Mail* reported, she 'was free and was being embraced outside the gate of Pudu Jail by her husband. Her father and mother . . . were also there to welcome her. Mrs. Proudlock was not attired in prison clothes, she having changed into clothes which her mother had forwarded . . . Nobody save her relatives were present at her release. She was in a highly nervous condition and, to avoid the possibility of a breakdown, she was advised to retire at once on her arrival at her destination.'

The day after her release, Mrs Proudlock did something rather unusual for a woman of her supposedly reclusive nature: she agreed to be interviewed by the *Malay Mail*. As described by the paper's reporter, she was very pale and had lost a lot of weight but, that aside, he said, she looked 'considerably brighter and more cheerful than at any period during her appearance in court'. Mrs Proudlock, ever conscious of the figure she cut, had dressed for the occasion in a cream-coloured suit.

Ethel told the *Mail* that she would soon be leaving for Penang where, after a short rest, she planned to sail for England. Though she had been given just four days in which to wind up her affairs, she made no mention of being under any pressure. She was going to London, she said, because she needed a complete change if she was ever to regain her health.

'It may not be generally known that as soon as the death sentence was passed on me I was placed in the condemned cell. I was placed on a prison diet and ordered to wear prison clothes . . . I was allowed permission to see particular friends, but was not able to speak to them through the iron bars of my cell. How I must have looked I cannot say.'

Her mental health became so precarious, she said, there

were fears she might do herself a violence: 'I was watched day and night . . . I was even denied the use of a knife with which to cut food.'

She continued to protest her innocence: 'In spite of the fate hanging over me, I felt myself justified absolutely in the act I had committed. The horrors of my imprisonment were intensified because I had not the knowledge that I was suffering for my sin.'

Though her gaolers had shown her every consideration, she described her time in prison as 'truly wretched. I can only say I have the deepest feeling of gratitude towards all those of every race' who extended their sympathy.

In Penang, the *Mail* reported a few days later, Mrs Proudlock stayed with friends. Though who they might have been is hard to say. Ethel, at this point, cannot have had many friends. People had begun to understand the problems she had caused. She had become a pariah, and the morning she left KL, there was no crowd of well-wishers at the railway station to see her off; no farewell toasts; no tears; no promises to stay in touch. Wishing perhaps to deter the curious, the authorities had taken the precaution of keeping her plans a secret.

There were no well-wishers, either, in Penang a week later when Mrs Proudlock, accompanied by Dorothy, her daughter, stood on Swettenham Pier, waiting to board the *Hidachi Mars*, a ship bound for Tilbury and flying the Japanese flag. Malaya heaved a sign of relief when the ship weighed anchor. It had rid itself, or so it thought, of a major headache.

Five days later, Mrs Proudlock reached Colombo where 'she was met on board by friends and went ashore with her child'. On 22 August, and looking 'somewhat thin', she reached England, then experiencing that rare phenomenon, a drought. When asked by a reporter to discuss her trial and incarceration, she declined. Nothing could compel to her to talk about it, she said; it was something she wished to forget. She did say, though, that she had returned to England in order to recuperate and that, while there, she would be staying with relatives. 'I hope that Mr. Proudlock will be able to join me here in a few months' time. But at present we cannot be sure of that.'

Had she plans to return to Malaya at some point? Mrs Proudlock really couldn't say. For the time being, she said, her only plan was to get some rest.

4

A Man on a Mission

There was no rest, however, for William Proudlock. Back in KL, his problems had begun to compound. Throughout that summer he soldiered on, running VI, drinking at the club occasionally, turning up at St Mary's – to see him, people said, one would think nothing had happened: that there had never been a murder; that Ethel had gone to England on holiday; that William Steward had never existed.

Proudlock was unlikely to have been that self-deluding. And even if he were, it could not have been for long because on 10 October, Bennett Shaw, VI's headmaster, returned from leave. Intending, perhaps, to tell him of Steward's death, Proudlock had gone to the station to meet him, but Shaw, it turned out, was aware of the murder, having read of it in the British papers (the London press dubbed it 'the murder on the verandah'). Doubtless he was appalled – not only because he liked the Proudlocks, but because of the opportunity it gave England's moralists to revive a familiar charge: without Mrs Grundy to keep an eye on them, the British abroad lived lives of depravity and dissolution.

Ten days later, the school marked Shaw's return by honouring him with a concert. The *Mail*, lavish with its praise as usual, declared the event a huge success. The paper particularly enjoyed a suite of English folk songs with piano accompaniment. Only in passing is it mentioned that the pianist was William Proudlock. Poor man. He can only have played with heavy heart. In the week and half since Shaw's return, the headmaster and he had had a chat during which Shaw explained that his presence at the school had become an embarrassment. Playing 'Greensleeves' that night, Proudlock knew his days were numbered. On 24 October, VI made it official; Proudlock had resigned his post, it was announced, and would be returning to England in the very near future.

Before he went anywhere, however, he had to endure yet another ordeal: a charge of libel brought against him by his former friend, Detective-Inspector Wyatt. The action had its origins in a letter Proudlock wrote to a London weekly called *M.A.P.* (*Mostly About People*), in which he castigated the Selangor government for what he said was the highly irregular manner in which his wife's trial had been conducted.

Though Proudlock's writing style is brisk and forthright, the letter clearly was composed in haste. Several words are misspelled, the Bible is misquoted, and his signature – hurried and careless; hardly more than a scrawl – looks as if it were penned by a child. (In the excerpts that follow, the spelling has been corrected.) Proudlock begins with an explanation. He was writing to the magazine, he said, to call 'the attention of the British public to the state of things in [Malaya] which I feel sure every rightminded Britisher will heartily condemn. The press out here has apparently been unable to induce the authorities to abandon trial by assessors in favour of trial by jury and so, off my own bat, I am going to see what I can do in the way of moving the authorities at Home.' He was not optimistic, he said. The London government knew little of the state of things in the FMS, so little that 'one feels inclined to say with Elijah "Either they are talking or peradventure they sleep and must be awaked."' (The quotation, from the first book of Kings, chapter 18, verse 27, reads: 'And it came to pass at noon, that Elijah mocked them, and said, Cry aloud: for he is a god; either he is talking, or he is pursuing, or he is in a journey, or peradventure he sleepeth, and must be awaked.')

Proudlock claimed that two men refused to sign the petition praying for a pardon for his wife, one giving as his reason that all women are unchaste, the other that all women are liars. 'These men might have been assessors,' he wrote. 'In Scotland (recently), it was necessary to employ a jury in a case about a pearl necklace, but out here in a case where the life of a human being is at stake, we can manage with two assessors who are allowed to mix with their fellow men while the trial is proceeding.'

Then, 'for the benefit of any poor devil who may be called upon to suffer the awful agony of mind my poor young wife went through', Proudlock lists a number of irregularities any one of which today would almost certainly result in a mistrial.

1. The assessors were not only friends, they were business associates which meant, he said, that, for all practical purposes, there was only one assessor at the trial.

2. During the six-day hearing, the assessors, instead of being sequestered, mixed freely, not only with members of the public, but with police officers and lawyers, and witnesses for the prosecution. This, Proudlock said, was highly improper and raised questions about their objectivity. (The chief secretary of the FMS would later defend the assessors. Their behaviour 'had the appearance of wrong,' he said, 'but I can-

not think they were discussing the case. I have no hesitation in describing both of them as imbued with a high sense of honour.')

3. While his wife was being tried for murder, the chief commissioner of police had approached a man in the Selangor Club and had offered to bet him 'five, ten or anything he liked that she (Mrs Proudlock) would be strung up'. (The chief commissioner would later receive a reprimand, the government arguing that demoting him would 'only add to the further public washing of excessively soiled linen'.)

Proudlock claimed as well – and this was the charge that Wyatt said questioned his integrity and resulted in his suing for gross and malicious libel – that the detective-inspector had beaten Proudlock's servants because they refused to incriminate his wife.

'I feel sure', Proudlock finished, 'that all who read this will agree that things out here are far too slack and that no person – white, black or yellow – be tried by less than twelve *sound* men even if they have to be imported from England.'

At 10.30 a.m. on 31 October, the trial began with H. N. Ferrers, Wyatt's counsel, describing Steward's murder as 'the most painful episode in the annals of crime in this country'. It was also, he said significantly, a case that everyone hoped had been closed. To the charge of libel, Ferrers now seemed to be adding another: with these frivolous accusations, William Proudlock was opening old wounds and prolonging Malaya's agony.

Ferrers then proceeded to paint the defendant as a radical – something he clearly was not. When Proudlock wrote to *M.A.P.*, he said, he was a man on a mission, a man whose purpose was 'to reform the very state of things as they existed in KL'. Proudlock was not present to hear himself characterized like this. For thirty minutes, the trial had proceeded without him – in itself irregular, one would have thought. All apologies, he arrived in court half an hour late.

Ferrers said Wyatt denied ever having assaulted the defendant's cook and 'boy'. The charge was not just without foundation; it was unfair. The detective was a friend of Mrs Proudlock's and had demonstrated as much by waiting seven days before imprisoning her and then going 'to considerable pains to assure her comparative comfort'.

According to Proudlock, Ferrers said, the 'boy' was asked if he had seen his master practising with the revolver on the day of the murder, and when he said he had not – that he'd only *heard* the shots – Wyatt is alleged to have struck him six times in the face.

Ferrers said the charge against Wyatt was intended as a preemptive strike. Mrs Proudlock's lawyers knew there had been intimacy and improper communication between her and Steward, and that were the matter to be pursued, her servants were likely to incriminate her. That's why the charge of beating had been concocted – to deprive any fresh evidence of its value by suggesting it had been coerced.

Mrs Proudlock had abandoned her appeal, Ferrers suggested, not as she had said because the strain would prove too much for her, but because she and her lawyers knew that the evidence against her was overwhelming and that 'the only chance of getting the lady off was by means of appealing to public sentiment'. This was done by representing her 'as a poor, persecuted, young and modest woman'.

On the witness stand, Proudlock claimed that Wyatt had asked his 'boy' if he had ever carried notes between Ethel and Steward, and that Wyatt became angry when the boy said he hadn't.

Proudlock also testified that Wyatt, asked by E. A. S. Wagner, Ethel's lawyer, if he had struck the servants, admitted that he had, saying: 'I had to straighten them up a bit. Cookie, the old fool, couldn't tell whether the lights were on or not.'

Wyatt then seemed to regret his candour, telling Wagner that were he ever to repeat this, the detective would bring a dozen witnesses to testify that he had not touched either of them. 'Do you think I am such a fool as to put my neck in a noose for a damn China man?'

Proudlock told the court that he'd written to *M.A.P.* because he had a duty to his wife. 'I believe that many things out here are slack, and I wanted to bring the things I knew about to the notice of the British public.'

Cross-examined by Ferrers, Proudlock denied being married when he and Ethel were wed in 1907. He had arrived in Malaya in 1901, he said, and for a time afterwards had lived with a Chinese woman – the mother of one of his pupils. Asked if he had continued seeing this woman after marrying Ethel, he admitted that he had.

While living with him, he said, the Chinese woman had had some jewellery stolen. He estimated its value at $1,500.

FERRERS: Wasn't it speculated that you had stolen it?
PROUDLOCK: That speculation was false.
FERRERS: After the jewellery was lost, weren't diamonds seen in your possession?
PROUDLOCK: Yes, but they were not part of the jewellery stolen.

Proudlock said the story that he was the thief had been put about by a European who later sent him a letter in which he withdrew the charge. While VI's acting headmaster, he had been responsible for large sums of money, and no one – with the exception of the letter-writer – had ever accused him of being dishonest.

Bennett Shaw, who had worked with Proudlock for ten years

and may have known him better than anyone, said the defendant had never told him anything but the truth. Proudlock's reputation for probity was a matter of record, he said; he considered him an honourable and upright man.

Shaw was not alone in that opinion. On 24 April 1907, the school's masters and boys hosted an entertainment at which Proudlock was the guest of honour. The programme consisted of 'musical items' and scenes from *The Merchant of Venice*, 'but the chief interest of the evening', said the *Mail*, 'centred on the speeches and presentations made to Mr Proudlock in view of his forthcoming marriage and departure on leave'. It was an emotional two hours. In speech after speech, Proudlock was praised for his commitment and dedication, his boundless energy, and his enormous decency. The school owed him a huge debt of gratitude, he was told, and there was no one – teacher or pupil – who did not hold him in the highest regard.

After being presented with three 'purses of gold' – one each from the students, the old boys, and the staff – Proudlock said his five years at the school had been so pleasant and so interesting, he was looking forward to resuming his duties in January. Shaw wound up the proceedings by wishing him 'a good holiday and all happiness in his matrimonial venture'. He then called for three cheers for Mr Proudlock and his future bride 'which were given with great enthusiasm'.

On the stand, Wyatt denied telling Wagner he had beaten the servants. Wagner, he said, had invented the conversation. As for his treatment of Mrs Proudlock, he said his consideration sprang from an awareness of the grief and trouble she was going through.

In a summation that lasted almost four hours – at one point Mr Justice Innes had to plead with him to hurry up – T. H. T. Rogers, Proudlock's counsel, said his client was convinced that, had his wife been tried by a jury, she would never have been convicted. 'Twelve manly men would never have stood by and seen a defenceless woman accused as she was.' Proudlock saw trial by assessors as inherently unfair and had written to *M.A.P.* in the hope that public pressure would convince the Home Office to abolish it.

Rogers referred to Mrs Proudlock as 'a defenceless woman suffering the deepest agony, charged with murder and separated from her defenceless child and with little evidence to support the charges. The conviction stood and would be a stigma that would keep to her during the rest of her life . . . The world was a cold, censorious place and nothing delighted the general public better, apparently, than something disastrous happening to one of their more unfortunate neighbours.'

On 11 November Mr Justice Innes found for the plaintiff. Proudlock, he said, had imperilled the reputation and the future of an officer. 'That officer now leaves the court with his reputation unsullied and with a claim to enjoy the same confidence from his superiors as before.' Proudlock was ordered to pay $300 and costs.

Even though he found for Wyatt, Innes admitted to admiring Proudlock. He gave his evidence, Innes said, 'in a straightforward and manly way and with self-control under trying conditions. The attacks upon his character entirely failed to weaken his credibility.' He seems as well to have felt some sympathy for him, going so far as to suggest extenuating circumstances. Before writing to *M.A.P.*, Innes said, Proudlock had had to endure 'the unspeakable horror of knowing that his wife's reputation was besmirched by the vilest rumours which he described in his evidence as filthy lies'.

Less than three weeks later, William Proudlock left KL to join his wife in England. His departure was a sad one. He loved the city and believed that he had given it much. It had been his intention to spend his life there, and though he spoke of coming back, he must have known that this was now impossible. Proudlock departed the capital of the Federated Malay States on 21 November 1911. He never returned.

Of the two photographs of William Proudlock I have been able to find one is especially revealing. It's a picture of him with members of VI's First Eleven, one of the football teams he played for. A small, slight man, he had a compact head (an acorn comes to mind) and his hair is shorn almost to the scalp. There is a suggestion of the monk about him; it is easy to imagine him wearing a cowl. Seated in the middle of the group, he seems to sprawl slightly, as if to give an impression of indifference. But it is only an impression. Proudlock's arms are folded so tightly across his chest, he might have been trying to staunch a wound. And his eyes: they engage the camera directly, but there's a wariness about them. Hard as he tries to look insouciant, Proudlock has the air of a man all too conscious that he doesn't measure up.

This must have caused him much distress because measuring up – mixing with others on equal terms; being accepted – was very important to him. While in KL, he worked tirelessly to make a good impression, though he would doubtless have denied it. In addition to after-hours tutoring, the piano recitals and the musical at-homes, he was a gymnastics instructor, coached the choir at St Mary's, was president of the Selangor State Band and a lieutenant in the fire brigade. (In a competition for firemen in August 1909, Proudlock's team won the Cape Hill Cup for best over-all performance, and the Selangor Government Cup for its skill in the four-men engine drill. Proudlock also took first place in the ladder competition, completing a complicated set of manoeuvres in a record time of 38 seconds.) And there was more: he belonged to the Malay State Volunteer Rifles – a group Winstedt considered to be very coarse. 'I can enjoy a witty story of the smoking-room type,' he said. 'But I have never been able to discover why volunteer canteens must be regaled by cold indecencies that should upset the gorge even of Dan the lavatory-man.'

The son of a millwright, Proudlock was born on 18 April 1880, and received his education, not at Eton like some in Malaya, but at a state school in Whittlesford, Cambridgeshire. In KL, where social credentials mattered, Proudlock had none to speak of, but that was of no account, he told himself. (There are times when he strikes one as very naïve.) He would prove himself in other ways. All those good deeds would redeem him. (He was an inveterate volunteer. When the Casuals, another football team, was founded in April 1910, Proudlock agreed to act not just as secretary, but as treasurer as well.)

During his trial for libel, Rogers referred to his client as a manly man. Proudlock would have been very proud. In Malaya in the early 1900s, to describe a man as manly – the tautology aside – was the ultimate compliment. The term had its origins in Muscular Christianity, a movement born in the 1850s whose aim was to re-invigorate British manhood. Muscular Christianity – its adherents preferred to be called manly Christians – emerged at a time when many believed that England had lost its way. Industrialization had made the country complacent and self-indulgent, people said; the masculine, Anglo-Saxon values of the rural gentry – values that had served England well in the past – were in eclipse.

In manly Christianity's major texts – *Westward Ho!* and *Tom Brown's Schooldays* are the most important – Charles Kingsley and Thomas Hughes proposed redeeming Britain by merging vigour with virtue. Men were encouraged to engage in athletics, the belief being that prowess on the playing field – in some way that was never fully explained – produced not just physical health, but spiritual health as well. As Victorian England saw him, the manly Christian was one who feared God and thought nothing of a 10-mile walk before sitting down to breakfast.

Manly Christianity proved hugely influential. It engendered the games culture that came to dominate the public schools where it also bred anti-intellectualism. (The boy who knew Virgil by heart ran a poor second to one who had earned his Flannels.) It informed as well the New Imperialism of the late 1890s, Joseph Chamberlain's call to Britain to go forth and civilize the barbarian. (The scout movement was founded in 1908 when the New Imperialism was at its height.)

Manly Christianity did not remain Christian for very long. While the public schools were full of vigour, they were rarely full of virtue. (In some, cheating, especially at exams, was endemic.) And while the New Imperialism spoke much of raising up those who dwelt in darkness, an altogether more immediate concern was raising a profit. As Cecil Rhodes once put it, imperialism was philanthropy plus a 5 per cent dividend on investment.

By 1911, Muscular Christianity as a spiritual force was running out of steam. Even its terms had been secluarized. Now the manly Christian was merely a manly man but, even reduced like this, he had much to recommend him. He was resolute; he was resourceful; he was chivalrous; he loved adventure – all qualities Proudlock embodied.

A spirit of adventure had brought Proudlock to Malaya. After being awarded a teacher's certificate by the English Board of Education, he seems to have languished for a while, studying drawing and physiography in London and joining the Isle of Man Singing Guild. Then, one day in 1900, his attention was drawn to an advertisement in *The Times.* A Mr Bennett Shaw was in London and wished to speak to candidates interested in teaching at the Victoria Institution in KL.

Proudlock, not yet twenty-one, landed the job and left for Malaya almost immediately. England would have seemed a little cramped for someone of his ambition. Here was a chance to escape his modest origins.

Proudlock flourished in KL and proved himself a first-rate teacher. (Why else would Shaw make him his deputy?) As acting headmaster, he earned a salary of $4,000 a year – more than enough to provide him and his family with a comfortable living. (Shaw returned to KL in 1901 with more than a new teacher; he also brought along a portrait of Queen Victoria, a gift from the monarch herself. After introducing Proudlock to the assembled boys, Shaw unveiled the painting 'which had been standing on an easel under cover of the Union Jack', a contemporary wrote. 'The customary three cheers were shouted and the ceremony ended.')

Manly man that he was, Proudlock did not give in easily. When he played for VI's First Eleven, it was the second-worst team in the Selangor Association Football League. In 1909, VI played nine games of which it won two, drew two and lost five. Not a sterling record by any standard, but Proudlock always played his heart out. In June of that year, VI took on Klang Malays in a game that, for much of its course, was undistinguished. (The *Mail* blamed this on the roughness of the ground and the fact that 'the ball was somewhat out of shape'.) The match was in its closing stages and still tied at nil–nil when Proudlock, 'running down with the ball, was floored by the two (Klang) backs, but had the presence of mind to kick the ball into the net whilst he was on the ground'. He was not a man who liked to lose.

Something of an idealist, he genuinely believed that by writing to *M.A.P.* the inherent decency of the British public would be stirred and wrongs would be set right. He hadn't counted on their apathy. The passion the New Imperialism had inspired was on the wane now, replaced by a feeling – understandable in the wake of the Boer War – that the empire had become an encumbrance. Worse, some said, it was an expense, drawing away resources that might better have been spent at home. If the empire had availed Britain at all – beyond providing cheap sugar and inexpensive tea – few were aware of it. In most people's eyes, all the empire did was sunder families, sending men to places they'd never heard of and from which, increasingly, more and more of them did not return.

Was Proudlock, as his wife suggested, an agnostic? In all likelihood, yes, and while it may seem odd that an agnostic – someone who considered believers credulous – would coach a church choir and regularly attend Evensong, Proudlock's reasons were probably pragmatic. The British Resident attended Evensong and was said to keep a list of those who did not. Officials and quasi-officials (Proudlock was one of the latter) could not hope to get ahead if they did not go to church. The godless had a choice: they could bend their principles or stick to their guns and languish in the same dull job for years.

For a time, KL had a lot of sympathy for Proudlock. Those few who still considered Ethel innocent naturally felt for him; but so, as well, did many of those who did not. Give the man credit, they said; he'd stood by his wife. He was steadfast. Too steadfast, others countered, but even these admitted to a grudging admiration. He was a fool, no doubt about it; but a loyal one. You had to give him that.

So why did KL abandon him? His great mistake was to embarrass those in authority. In Malaya, this was the Great Taboo, and those who violated it paid a heavy price. In October 1927, the governor of the Straits Settlements denounced as hysterics two young doctors who protested the appalling conditions at Penang Hospital. The hospital had been the target of criticism for years. As early as 1910, a

Penang newspaper had denounced it as a death-trap. And now, finally, a visiting committee had proposed pulling it down. Still the government did nothing, and the doctors had had enough. Those in authority 'were suffering from that tired feeling during office hours', they complained, and suggested that what the government needed was 'the return of the broom and a clean sweep'. Their temerity cost them dear. One was sent to Kedah – considered at the time the back of beyond – and the other, a first-rate surgeon, was demoted. The effect in both cases was to ruin their careers.

Anyone who wanted to criticize – and cared for his future – had to chose his words judiciously. Officials had awfully thin skins and did not much like being called to account. Proudlock, though, did more than merely criticize; he called into question the integrity of the entire colonial administration. Things were slack, he wrote – a term which, while it sounded innocent enough, was understood to mean that the administration was arrogant, that it no longer considered itself accountable, that it felt it could do much as it pleased.

Even worse, Proudlock had raised these questions in the English press. This had ceased being a domestic matter, the sort of thing that might be hushed up. Proudlock had bypassed not just the government of the FMS, but the government of the Straits Settlements as well and had addressed himself directly to the British public. By doing so, he offended, and threatened the careers of, senior officials in both jurisdictions. These people were expected to run competent administrations or, failing that, to do nothing likely to embarrass London. Proudlock, who was something of an innocent and may not have realized the extent of his effrontery, had made some powerful enemies.

Later, he would regret his impetuosity. Asked during his trial why, instead of involving the British press, he had not asked the Malayan authorities to investigate his allegations, he said: 'Thinking it over quietly now, I think it would have been the best course. At the time, I did not give it a thought.'

In what today would be called damage control, Arthur Young, High Commissioner for the FMS, sent the Colonial Office an editorial that had run in the *Singapore Free Press.* It described Proudlock's letter to *M.A.P.* as a 'concoction of insinuation' with 'the main intention to throw mud at the judicial, magisterial and police administration in the FMS and to impugn the fairmindedness of the justice who presided at the trial, the assessors . . . assisting him, the prosecution and the medical witness.'

'In my opinion,' Young added, 'this is a very fair summary of the letter.'

Whether or not Proudlock's charges were valid hardly mattered now. It was enough that he had made them, and the response was immediate. On 20 September, he was summoned before the chief secretary of the FMS and ordered to give an account of himself.

Proudlock, demonstrating the tenacity that was his hallmark, refused to be cowed – though doubtless every effort was made to make the interview as intimidating as possible. Asked to explain the allegations he had made in his letter, he proceeded to do just that. Everything, he insisted, was true.

Still oblivious to the damage he had done himself, Proudlock now wrote to Government House in Singapore asking that his name be submitted to the secretary of state 'as a candidate for employment in the education department of the government service of one of the colonies or protectorates administered by the Colonial Office.

'My sole reason for making this application', he said, 'is that I do not think it advisable for my wife who, a short time ago, was granted a free pardon after being sentenced to death, to return to this country.'

The authorities would have seen this as more effrontery, and a decision was made: Proudlock would have to be removed. On 21 September, the Colonial Office wrote to the government in Singapore asking if the officers mentioned in the *M.A.P.* letter should be encouraged to seek damages for libel. In his reply, R. J. Wilkinson informed London that, 'before the receipt of your dispatch, Inspector Wyatt had applied for permission to take legal proceedings against Mr. Proudlock . . . [and] permission was granted'.

Wilkinson added that the chief secretary of the FMS had also considered whether the other officers involved should not seek redress, but had decided 'that there was no necessity for them to do so and that it might appear oppressive for action to be taken'.

Shortly afterwards, the Secretary of State for the Colonies informed the governor in Singapore that, while he did not think pressure should be brought to bear on VI's trustees 'with a view to the removal of Mr. Proudlock from his present position', he was of the opinion that Proudlock's 'further employment at the Victoria Institution is not desirable'.

This sounds awfully like an official trying to have it both ways: declining to take an action that might later embarrass him while, at the same time, leaving his subordinates in no doubt as to what he wanted done. Certainly, that was how the governor read it because, two weeks later, William Proudlock was unemployed.

Proudlock resigned under duress and then only after being assured by not one but *two* senior British officials that the Colonial Office would find him another job. The Colonial Office did not; it did not so much as try. The two officials would later claim that he had misunderstood them. And in one sense he had: he had taken them for men of their word.

This was not the only betrayal that Proudlock suffered. He was an outcast now. It became an act of courage to have anything to do with him, and many weren't up to it. In some ways his wife fared better, despite the fact that she had committed murder. In official eyes, Proudlock had done something infinitely worse: he had exposed British claims to value decency and fairness above all else as a sham.

5

The Role of a Lifetime

The description of Mrs Proudlock on the night of the murder – her hair disordered, eyes starting from her head, and gurgling the words 'Blood! Blood!' – brings to mind another Ethel, this one in V. S. Pritchett's novel *Mr Beluncle*: 'Then Ethel appeared . . . with her hair dividing over her cheeks and looking from it like a savage peeping in terror from an old tent.'

To the extent that she has one, Ethel's archetype might be Euripides' Phaedra. Like Ethel, Phaedra was a victim of frustrated passion. Like Ethel, she was spurned by the man she loved. Like Ethel, she was responsible for killing him. Like Ethel, she claimed that she'd been violated. Of the two of them, though, Mrs Proudlock proved the more resilient. She escaped the gallows, while Phaedra, her crime weighing on her, 'within a hanging rope she noosed her neck'.

A parallel might also be drawn between Ethel's husband, William, and Phaedra's husband, Theseus. Both end up being ostracized, and for much the same reason: they were gullible. (Artemis berates Theseus for 'Believing the lies of a wife that told thee / Things all unproven . . .') The price they pay is similar as well. Will is made to return to England, a country he would soon consider hell. And Theseus? 'Go now,' Artemis tells him, 'and hide in the darkness of Hades.'

In Maugham's story 'The Letter', the character based on Ethel is Leslie Crosbie, a woman 'in the early thirties, a fragile creature, neither short nor tall, and graceful rather than pretty. Her wrists and ankles were very delicate, but she was extremely thin, and you could see the bones of her hands through the white skin, and the veins were large and blue. Her face was colourless, slightly sallow, and her lips were pale . . . She had a great deal of light brown hair, and it had a slight natural wave; it was the sort of hair that with a little touching-up would have been very pretty, but you could not imagine that Mrs Crosbie would think of resorting to any such device. She was a quiet, pleasant, unassuming woman. Her manner was engaging, and if she was not very popular it was because she suffered from a certain shyness . . . [I]n her own house, with people she knew, she was in her quiet way charming.'

Maugham is creating a dichotomy: on the one hand, Leslie frail and gentle, a woman of breeding; on the other, Leslie the monster; the *femme fatale*. This is how he describes her when, as the story closes, she lets her guard slip: 'Her face was no longer human, it was distorted with cruelty, and rage and pain. You would never have thought that this quiet, refined woman was capable of such fiendish passion . . . It was not a face, it was a gibbering, hideous mask.'

How closely did Ethel resemble her fictional counterpart? When Maugham wrote 'The Letter', he did all the usual things a writer does to avoid prosecution: he changed crucial details, altering names and ages, professions and locales. The outcome was changed as well. In Maugham's telling, Leslie Crosbie is acquitted, the spectator gallery breaking into applause when the verdict is read, and the judge congratulating her on being a free woman again. These touches aside, however, 'The Letter' sticks by and large to the facts.

Ethel did not have brown hair; hers was blonde. And unlike Mrs Crosbie, whose appearance did not matter to her, Ethel was a vain creature whose chief delight was buying clothes. But the other particulars fit – which makes one wonder if Wagner supplied Maugham with an especially good description or if the writer found a photograph, one that has since gone missing.

Like Leslie, Ethel was a small, guarded woman who kept largely to herself. The *Mail*, which did not hesitate to tell its readers when Mr Birch was feeling 'sickly' or Mr Hubback had sprained a knee, rarely mentioned her. Mrs Proudlock turned up at the club occasionally and played tennis when she could, but, that aside, moved little in the public eye. She spent most of her time at home doing what women did in the early 1900s: making cushions and antimacassars – she was handy with a needle – writing letters and reading *Punch*. When this palled, there were shopping sprees to relieve the tedium. Mrs Proudlock spent so much time in John Little's millinery department, some people thought she worked there.

She was an able hostess. While Ethel was constrained in public, on her own turf she was quite another person. Surrounded by her cushions and her samplers and enjoying the deference due to her as the lady of the house, she found it in her to relax, going so far on occasion – after the requisite coaxing, of course; Mrs Proudlock loved to tease – as to treat her guests to a song or two from *The Pirates of Penzance*.

To all appearances, the Proudlocks were a happy couple. Goodman Ambler who, until they moved to Shaw's bungalow, shared a house with them for six months, said 'they lived on most affectionate terms. I never saw Mrs Proudlock do anything which would cause her husband to complain. She was extremely kind and gentle.'

Ethel had few friends of her own. Most of those who came to the house were associates of her husband's: other teachers, fellow footballers, members of the fire brigade. The Proudlocks were not well connected. As in other parts of the empire, the British in KL were organized platonically: like was expected to stick with like. Will and Ethel did not consort with the upper echelons. They did not hunt or play polo; they did not go to dinner parties or attend the better weddings. They were minor figures, the sort of people who lurk on the edges of photographs, and most of those they mixed with were minor figures, too.

Ethel was probably Eurasian, a person having European and Asian blood. Certainly, this is how she was described by Mabel Marsh, the much-respected American who ran the Methodist Girls' School and for whom Ethel briefly worked. Her birth certificate also suggests as much. Robert Charter is listed as Ethel's father, but there is no mention of any mother – a practice not uncommon when a child was of mixed race. Something Hippolytus said comes to mind: 'God save all those I love from bastardy.'

Ethel, whose lack of candour sometimes bordered on secrecy, rarely mentioned the ambiguity surrounding her birth. For years, she even kept it from her husband. It seems a curious decision, unless it means that she did not trust him. Questioned at his libel trial about his wife's 'actual' parentage, Proudlock said that rumours that her mother might be Asian reached his ears only *after* he married: 'I sent my wife to Mrs Charter who said, "I am your mother." At any rate, that was the answer brought back to me. Charter said, "I'm prepared to swear I am her father."'

That was the answer brought back to me. What could that mean? Did he not trust her, either?

Ethel and William married on 25 April 1907 and honeymooned in England. While there, they spent several months at 7 Adelaide Square in Bedford, where they may have rented rooms. It was there, on 30 January 1908, that their daughter, Dorothy, was born. But the birth certificate raises questions. The birth was not registered until 6 March – a delay of nearly six weeks. This was unusual, but there was something else. Customarily, it was the father who registered the birth of a child. In this case, the birth was registered by Ethel. On 6 March, Will had been back in KL for over a month, having left England at the beginning of January – *before* the baby's putative birth.

I find this hard to believe. Proudlock was much too conscientious, much too responsible to abandon his sickly wife a month before the expected delivery of their first child. It simply wasn't in him. When Ethel gave birth, Proudlock, surely, was with her.

Dorothy, one suspects, was born some time in late November, which would explain the Proudlocks' extraordinary behaviour at their wedding. In the early 1900s, weddings in KL were elaborate affairs. The marriage of Walker Reed and Frieda Heuer on 2 February 1910 was like many others of the period. Though neither the bride nor the groom was socially prominent, several leading citizens were present. The event was covered by the *Malay Mail*, the list of wedding gifts alone filling nearly a column of type. (The Proudlocks, making a rare appearance at one of these events, contributed a set of silver bon-bon dishes.)

The bride's ensemble – a gown of lace over silk, and a white tulle veil set off by orange blossoms – had been purchased in London; and the state band, at great expense, had been hired to play the Wedding March. For the reception, guests adjourned to a garden where a marquee had been raised. Lunch consisted of salmon and grouse and venison. And cases and cases of champagne. It was all very jolly, and afterwards there was dancing on the lawn. When it came time for the newly-weds to leave, the bride, after slipping away briefly, reappeared in a 'travelling dress of white *broderie anglaise* and a becoming burnt-straw hat trimmed with roses'. A friend had loaned the couple a car – in 1910 still something to marvel at – the back of which had been 'well-supplied with dilapidated footgear'. When the two drove off, they did so 'amidst a shower of confetti'.

By contrast, Ethel's wedding in St Mary's, at one o'clock on Tuesday, 25 April 1907, was a modest affair. The report in the *Mail* extended to just four paragraphs. With the exception of Bennett Shaw, there was no mention of any notables, which almost certainly means there weren't any, and no mention, either, of gifts, suggesting perhaps that those presents the couple *did* receive were modest.

Ethel cannot have enjoyed herself very much. For one thing, her father was absent, which would have upset her. He had gone to Ceylon a month earlier, intending to be back for the wedding, but had managed somehow to miss the boat. If not actually irresponsible, this at the very least smacks of carelessness. Few events are as important to a man as the marriage of a daughter. Is it possible that Charter did not like Ethel very much?

One doubts whether any of the Charters did. The elder of Mrs Proudlock's putative sisters lived in Colombo where she was often visited by her mother and her younger sister, but never by Ethel. This is strange. The British loved Ceylon – it was cooler than KL – and went there as often as they could. Ethel was delicate. She was often sick. A change of climate would have done her good. Why, then, did they never invite her along?

If, as seems likely, Ethel was illegitimate, her presence in that family can only have been a source of friction. In the circumstances, it seems extraordinary that Mrs Charter would agree to raise her at all – even if 'raising' meant little more than having her in the house. How they must have resented her. Through no fault of her own, those who should have loved Ethel the most saw her only as an interloper.

It is possible, too, that as much as he disliked Ethel, Charter disliked Will even more. Though he had a job of no great importance at the Public Works Department, Charter was something of a figure in KL. In addition to running the fire brigade, he was an amateur horticulturist. (He was among the first in the FMS to cultivate the Calcutta guava.) He had another distinction: he was an excellent shot – most seasons, it was he who bagged the first snipe – and, in gun-mad KL, a skill like that could take a man far. While Charter's background was not much more distinguished than Proudlock's, he was well connected, and this had made him something of a snob. Proudlock was a teacher at a time when teaching did not carry much status. The early 1900s, said Richard Winstedt, were 'the happy-go-lucky days when a knowledge of irregular verbs and an aptitude for games were considered adequate equipment for a schoolmaster'. As ambitious as he was, Charter may have wished for more.

In her father's absence, Ethel was given away by C. R. Cormac; H. J. Markes acted as best man; and Marjorie Charter, Ethel's sister, was the bridesmaid. (Markes was an assistant engineer in the Public Works Department, and Cormac was a supervisor in the Department of Posts and Telegraphs.) Signing the register afterwards, Ethel, then nineteen years old, entered under the heading 'occupation' the single word 'spinster'.

'The bride was dressed in a costume of electric blue with

handsome lace trimming and a white hat,' the *Mail* reported. 'The bridegroom was in a white suit with fire-brigade epaulettes, and members of the fire brigade in white suits and epaulettes lined up in the aisle on the entrance and departure of the bride and the bridegroom.

'After the ceremony, a reception was held at Casuarinas, Bluff Road, the residence of Mr. and Mrs. Charter. The bride and bridegroom left by the 3.15 train en route for England.'

It is curious that Ethel, always so alert to fashion's nuances, would have married in 'electric blue' instead of the customary white. That, alone, would have set tongues wagging. But odder still is this: the couple, who left St Mary's about 1.25 and would have reached Bluff Road around 1.40, must – if they caught the 3.15 train – have left for the railway station no later than half-past two. They spent less than an hour at their own wedding reception – an inauspicious way to start a marriage. There can hardly have been time for a toast.

Why the enormous hurry? If the ship they were taking to England left Penang on Wednesday, why didn't they marry on Monday? Or, if that was not possible, why wait till Tuesday afternoon? Why not Tuesday morning? For several weeks prior to the wedding, Ethel was seen little around KL. It is hard to escape a suspicion that, when she walked up the aisle on 25 April, the blushing bride was pregnant.

It was Ethel's wont to drop from view from time to time. When she felt poorly, she took to her bed and consumed large quantities of Dr Williams' Pink Pills, a popular remedy whose ads in the form of spurious case histories often appeared in the *Malay Mail.* 'Husband nerve-wrenched; wife dyspeptic,' goes one; 'How health was regained in a Rangoon home by the tonic treatment with over 20 years worldwide reputation as a guarantee.'

Proudlock testified at her murder trial that his wife was

anaemic – a not uncommon condition in pregnant women – and suffering from neuralgia when they married, and that, on the voyage back to England, 'I had to take her to the ship's doctor several times'. Nor had things improved when she returned to KL. Her anaemia was now as bad as ever, and her headaches, if anything, were even more severe.

When she ovulated, he said, she trembled and twitched so badly, she often had to stay in bed. At such times, she was acutely sensitive: 'She would frequently cry for very little and be inclined to take offence at what I should consider nothing.' For as long as he had known her, he added, his wife had been very nervous and was easily frightened.

On the stand, Ethel blamed some of her problems on Dorothy. The birth had been difficult, she said, and she had been in poor health ever since. (This was hardly fair to her daughter; Ethel had been claiming poor health for as long as anyone could remember.) Not everyone believed her. Witnesses for the prosecution described her as a hypochondriac, a selfish hysteric, a woman who craved attention and a skilled manipulator who feigned illness when faced with opposition.

Giving evidence at her trial, Dr McGregor described Ethel as a virtual invalid, a woman racked by pain and often confined to bed. The public prosecutor would have none of it. 'But she plays tennis,' Hastings Rhodes reminded him. McGregor was caught off guard and, for a moment, seemed lost for words. In the end, though, he had to agree.

Mrs Proudlock played tennis well and, in 1909, qualified for the annual tournament at the Selangor Club. Ethel signed up for the mixed-doubles, choosing as her partner C. G. Coleman, a colleague of her husband's. Coleman was another strong player, but the two did not do well and were eliminated in the early rounds. Ethel, though, did not lose heart. She continued playing tennis and continued improving her game until, quite suddenly, in early 1910 she dropped the sport altogether.

She also withdrew from the Selangor Ladies' Rifle Association. She had been a leading light in the SLRA for years and regularly attended its monthly spoon shoot. But in January 1910, she turned out for what was to be the last time, finishing thirteenth in a field of nineteen. (The other Charter girls, both older than Ethel, finished fourteenth and fifteenth.) It was a poor showing for Ethel; the previous September, she had finished first.

Two weeks after the January spoon shoot, Ethel landed a small part in *The Arcagettes*, a musical burlesque being produced by KL's amateur dramatic society. Rehearsals began almost immediately and lasted three months, which would explain her absence from the shoots in February, March and April. Yet Mrs Proudlock loved shooting and took pride in her marksmanship – something she shared with her father. Why did she not resume in May when *The Arcagettes* had closed and her time was once again her own?

It is true that, while living in KL, Ethel ventured out very little, but now, in April 1910 and until her re-emergence in Gilbert and Sullivan's *Trial by Jury* eleven months later, she seems to have gone to ground completely. Those who knew her speculated that something had happened to aggravate her health: either her anaemia had worsened or her headaches had returned. All wide of the mark, as it happened. In April 1910, Mrs Proudlock was feeling better than she had in years. She was in the throes of a passionate affair with William Steward.

She was also working for the first time. Having tired of making antimacassars, she had taken a job at the Methodist Girls' School. (Nominally a kindergarten teacher, her work consisted of making sure that no one wandered off and drowned in the river.) Though her husband would have had to give his consent, the decision was probably hers. A good Edwardian, Proudlock would not have approved of his wife working outside the home, but in this case he may not have had much choice. Ethel, at pains to impress her new lover, was spending more and more time – and more and more of her husband's money – in John Little's hat department. By agreeing to let her work, he may have hoped to avoid insolvency.

The Arcagettes was performed on three separate occasions, and the *Mail* reviewed all three, an indication that, in KL in 1910, theatre was a rare commodity. Ethel, a member of the chorus, played a shepherdess called Melodia and, that first night, was well received. 'The shepherds and shepherdesses showed signs of careful training,' said the *Mail* on 15 April. 'Generally speaking, they supported the principals exceedingly well . . . The shepherdesses, who all looked delightful, wore dresses of similar design in varied colourings with hats to match. Mrs Proudlock . . . wore a pink skirt with a bodice of green with a design of pink roses.'

This was as good as it got for Ethel. When *The Arcagettes* was reviewed again two days later, she was not mentioned – which cannot have pleased her very much because the other shepherdesses were. One – a Mrs Ebden – was 'the life and soul' of the chorus; another showed distinct promise; and a third was deemed outstanding. Of course, it may have been an oversight, but I doubt it. It is much more likely that Mrs Proudlock was not very good, and kindness alone prevented the critic from saying so.

The Arcagettes received its third performance on 30 April before an audience that included Sir John Anderson, the British High Commissioner. On this occasion, even the lively

Mrs Ebden failed to charm. 'It is not for our humble pen to criticize the chorus,' the *Mail* said. 'We will merely say that they all worked with a will.'

By now, word of the show had spread beyond KL, and the house that night was packed with planters and miners. Steward would almost certainly have been one of them. For one thing, KL was starved for entertainment; productions like this were few and far between. And for another, his affair with Mrs Proudlock was five months old at this point. The man was besotted, as infatuated with her as she with him. This was a big moment for her. It was only natural that he would want to share it.

Was it on his account that she 'worked with a will' that night? And what of him? Did he clap louder than he should have when she took her bows? Did he give himself away by jumping to his feet? One can imagine him, his thoughts on that green bodice with its pink roses as he headed back to Salak South afterwards. What an unfortunate man! He had no idea how unstable she was, no inkling of the danger he was in. But then how could he? No one knew. Not even Ethel herself.

The affair had begun the previous December when Proudlock and Wagner went to Hong Kong on business. (The nature of that business is nowhere specified.) In his absence, Proudlock had arranged that Markes, his best man, would look in on Ethel from time to time. She hated being alone, he said; it made her nervous. Actually, Ethel was more than nervous. She was terrified – lest Markes discover Steward and her in bed. Then she seems to have grown incautious because, two weeks later, she gave a dinner party. It was small and, in as much as her guests saw little of her that night, not very orthodox. Mrs Proudlock spent most of the evening with Steward, in the back seat of his car.

Their affair lasted some twelve months, during which time they trysted when and where they could. It was extraordinarily reckless of them. KL was small and full of busybodies. The risk of discovery was everywhere. Was this part of the appeal? Had Ethel tired of being meek? Did she see this fling as an act of self-assertion? Whatever her reasons, she took enormous risks: travelling to Steward's home – sometimes with her daughter – leaving her clothes in his bedroom, coupling under her husband's roof . . .

There was in her an element of self-destruction. At her trial, there were several moments when she came dangerously close to damning herself. When describing how Steward was alleged to have attacked her, she said he tried to drag her into the drawing room where there was 'a soft bed-couch'. Steward would not have known about that bed if, as she claimed, he was visiting the bungalow for the first time.

On another occasion, Sercombe Smith told Ethel that he thought her evidence far-fetched and asked, in effect, if she were telling the truth. This was her chance to protest her innocence but, inexplicably, she did not do so. In what amounted to a tacit admission of guilt, she said nothing.

As 1910 neared its end, Ethel was seeing less and less of Steward and, like Phaedra, by sickness faded, she wasted upon her bed. He had tired of her now and was rumoured to be seeing a Chinese woman. (The rumour was true. A month later, the two would be co-habitating.) In the view of Sercombe Smith, Steward's murder was not premeditated, but this is open to doubt. In March, Ethel approached Mabel Marsh and asked to have a few hours off. Her husband's birthday was coming up, and she wanted to buy him a present. She had decided on a gun, she said; the thing Will enjoyed more than anything was shooting crocodiles.

Proudlock was not a gun-lover. He was a gentle soul. For

recreation, he played piano. He wrote songs. Ethel, I suspect, bought that revolver, not for her husband's use, but for her own. As early as a month before the murder, she made a decision: if Steward refused to resume their relationship, she would kill him.

So much in Ethel's life reeked of deceit: her parentage, her wedding day, her health problems, her daughter's birth – Ethel Proudlock was chronically dishonest. People who saw her on the witness stand remarked on how self-possessed she looked, but she was a practised liar. Ethel had been dissembling all her life.

An aspiring actress, Ethel on stage was Ethel at her most content. Four weeks before the murder, she was back in the Town Hall in a production of *Trial by Jury*. This time, she was singled out for special mention. 'Mrs. Proudlock . . . as chief bridesmaid . . . led a chorus that ably supported the principals,' said the *Mail*, and 'added considerably to the success of the performance.'

Ethel felt vindicated. She had had her fill of small parts. Maybe now she would get a role that was worthy of her. A month later, she did: the lead in her own trial for murder. The toast of the town one moment; an accused killer the next. No wonder people were incredulous.

Only when the verdict was read did she realize the danger she was in. Until then, she seems to have enjoyed herself. She was in a tight corner, but she would rise to the occasion. This was what she had always wanted: a chance to shine; an opportunity to show her mettle.

Had she been a better actress, she might have pulled it off. Instead, she violated acting's first rule: never over-reach. Ethel on the stage was one thing; Ethel in the dock was another. As people testified against her, she pulled out all the stops. She rolled her eyes. She swooned. She clutched her brow. She gasped. She gazed about her imploringly. She wept.

Mrs Proudlock did what the guilty often do: she played for sympathy. Her mistake was to try too hard. Instead of the frightened and confused victim of circumstance she wanted to appear, much of the time she seemed merely calculating. As her performance in *The Arcagettes* had failed, so did this one, and for much the same reason: it did not convince.

II

Ethel's World

6

Foxtrots and Claret

When Will Proudlock returned to KL in 1908, the trip would have taken three to four weeks. Most people going to Malaya disembarked in Penang, with stops *en route* (depending on the shipping line) in Gibraltar, Marseilles, Malta, Trieste, Port Said, Djibouti, Aden, Bombay, Colombo and Rangoon.

If they could, people avoided Port Said. It was a coaling station, the dust so thick that passengers had to keep their portholes closed and all doors carefully sealed. It was also a den of iniquity, 'a hot imposthume', Winstedt said, 'lanced but not cured by British administration'. Its fly-blown lemonade didn't endear it to anyone, either. Djibouti, though, was even worse: 'a forlorn white-and-ochre settlement pitched in one of earth's waste places . . . [where] a loathsome crowd of deformed natives crawl round on hands and knees, pestering you with matches and pleading for alms.' For years afterwards, Winstedt said, he was visited by Djibouti in his worst nightmares.

Others sought to avoid Colombo, but this was for reasons of convenience. By disembarking in Bombay and crossing the sub-continent by rail, several days at sea could be saved. Travellers taking the train bought their tickets at Thomas Cook which had just opened an office in Bombay. 'Most useful people to deal with,' said an unidentified man writing in the *Mail* in 1911. But the journey itself, all forty-one hours of it, bordered on the dreary: 'In this part of India, the country is flat.' And there were hazards to contend with. In Bombay's railway station, the writer complained, his luggage was handled by 'dirty, untidy-looking ruffians'. The ticket collectors were little better. Most, he informs us, 'were of Eurasian stamp'.

Travellers were expected to provide their own bedding and toilet articles, but with a pillow and a rug purchased from Whiteaway, Laidlaw in Bombay, the *Mail*'s writer managed to make himself moderately comfortable. Tea was brought to the carriages both in the morning and the afternoon, and there was always plenty of iced water. The train lacked a dining car, however, forcing passengers to take their meals in station restaurants.

Once in Calcutta, one put up at the Grand Hotel, where most of the rooms were palatial. But caution was called for. If guests failed to impress the staff with their importance – if, in other words, they didn't stand on their dignity – they were likely to end up, as our writer did, 'in a very inferior, second-rate resthouse-sort-of room opening into the billiard room'.

The Grand was a great favourite with the Malaya set. In the lobby that first morning, the man from the *Mail* met so many friends, 'I began to wonder if I were in Calcutta or Kuala Lumpur.' One was Mrs Redfearn, who had recently appeared in *The Arcagettes* with Mrs Proudlock, and another was Dr E. A. O. Travers, bearing – for a reason not explained – a very large cake. Travers and the writer had a drink together and ended up spending the day at the races.

As someone whose means were limited, Proudlock is likely

to have travelled second class. (In 1908, a first-class fare from London to Penang cost about £50, a second-class one in the region of £30.) And as he was alone, he would have had to share a cabin. This was always a risk since few cared to spend three weeks in a cramped room with a total stranger. The *Mail* called this practice 'nothing more or less than a relic of barbarism' and predicted that 'a fortune [awaited] the first big steam ship line which makes up its mind to specialize in single-berth cabins at moderate rates'.

There were other indignities. Second-class passengers were required to dine at mid-day. (Those in first class *lunched* at mid-day and dined in the evening.) Many deemed the practice 'a stupid old custom' and accused shipping lines of reinforcing social distinctions. In 1909, the P & O agreed. Starting immediately, it said, *all* passengers would dine at eight o'clock. The *Mail* applauded the decision and said the company had removed 'one of the chief sources of complaint among the less affluent passengers'.

In other ways, however, the distinction between first- and second-class remained as strong as ever. In Maugham's story 'P. & O.', first-class passengers debate whether those in second class should be asked to their Christmas party. Many are of the view that an invitation would put the second-class passengers in a false position; that they would feel uncomfortable. Even worse, they were likely to get drunk and ruin the event for everyone. In the end, it is decided to extend an invitation anyway, after suggesting to the captain that he withhold his consent.

As well as distinction between classes, there was also distinction within classes. This was particularly evident in the dining room. With the exception of 'notables' – people such as well-to-do businessmen, generals and senior civil servants – who always ate with the captain, passengers took their meals at tables to which they were assigned when boarding. Who sat where and with whom was determined by the head waiter, a man whose knowledge of the British class system was *non-pareil.* George Bilainkin, editor of the *Straits Echo,* explained how the system worked: 'The man who parades in a tennis shirt, however clean and well pressed, under a blue serge suit . . . will be placed in the humblest category. But a man in a pair of flannels of unostentatious colour and shade, notwithstanding the tennis shirt, will be accorded the honour of inclusion in a higher group.' Not, though, if he happens to be wearing 'a screaming tie'. A man like this 'fell' at once, 'marked as a person of plebeian tastes'.

In second class, the trip was far from comfortable. The food was not good, the saloon was often crowded and, unless one read a lot, there was nothing much to do. For those with little money, it was also expensive. The shipping lines were ever 'augmenting' their fares. This might have been tolerable had it meant better service, but the opposite occurred. As prices rose, standards fell. The *Mail* complained that crews, especially on British boats, had become increasingly indifferent to 'the comfort and requirements of the work-a-day British passenger'.

Many people preferred to book with European shipping lines, giving as their reason the better service. On boats belonging to Norddeutscher Lloyd, for example, an orchestra performed during dinner, there were excellent health facilities, the crews spoke English and – *mirabile dictu* – the engine rooms did not smell. True, most of the passengers were German, but in and of itself that was not a problem. 'Germans who have travelled are generally more at home with English people than is the case with other Europeans,' said the man from the *Mail* in 1911, an opinion he no doubt disavowed when war broke out three years later. 'I am certain that, provided a conversation can be carried on, an Englishman soon finds himself more in sympathy with a German than with people of the Latin races.'

Not even Lloyd was perfect, though. Because most on board were German, the cuisine was German, too. By the third day out, English passengers had had their fill of schnitzel. (The writer admitted to preferring the P & O table.) Even worse was the indefatigable and ubiquitous brass band. Not even an odourless engine room could compensate for that.

Whether one travelled first class or second, the trip must have seemed inordinately long. People smoked a lot, played bridge, drank to excess and derived what amusement they could from observing their fellow passengers. When Winstedt went east for the first time in 1902, his shipmates included a young dandy ever splendid in frock-coat and silk hat, a French *vicomte* in riding breeches and white kid gloves, and an adolescent who drove everyone to despair by singing round the clock. ('Songs of Araby' was his special favourite.)

Desperate for something to do, people sometimes fell in love – though, usually, not for very long. Most were smart and made it a rule to have regained their senses long before the ship came in sight of Penang. Some, though, did not, and this made for complications – especially for women already engaged and going to Malaya for the purpose of getting married.

After three weeks at sea, it was a relief to reach Penang, which may explain the enthusiasm it inspired. A tiny island two miles off Malaya's coast, its admirers called it 'the pearl of the Orient'. James Abraham, an English ship's doctor arriving there in 1906, marvelled at how green everything was: 'The land rose precipitous from the water's edge, crag upon crag of naked rock . . . with here and there the white outlines of verandahed bungalows, perched perilously on the heights, which, half hidden in the verdure, rose higher and higher, and culminated finally in one great peak [Penang Hill] 2,700 feet above the sea.'

Most of those arriving in Penang for the first time had jobs in other parts of Malaya, but before crossing to the mainland, they spent a day on the island – a day that, with time, took on all the force of ritual: in the morning, a trip to the top of Penang Hill; in the afternoon, a stop in the Botanic Gardens; in the evening, dinner and dancing in the E & O Hotel. Before the funicular railway opened in 1923, those climbing the hill could do so on foot, on ponies, or in doolies, a variety of sedan chair suspended on bamboo poles and borne on the shoulders of Tamil labourers. The latter was the method preferred by ladies, and there was much grumbling when they reached the top about the discomfort they had had to endure.

In its own small way, that first day was emblematic. Penang Hill and the Botanic Gardens, with their sycamores and sloping lawns, looked like Wiltshire. And dinner in the E & O, where 'the chef was an expert from Geneva', might well have been a meal in London. Nothing too foreign here, if you were careful not to look very hard – and most of the British did not. Yet much about Penang *was* foreign. Not far from the E & O were opium dens and child prostitutes and one of the world's largest leper colonies. There was the Temple of the Azure Cloud with its population of deadly snakes, 'creeping over the altars and entwined upon the screens'. Even the Botanic Gardens were less bucolic than they seemed. Lurking among the oaks and willows were ipoh trees whose sap contained a virulent poison, and clumps of nibong palm, the stems of which were used as blow pipes.

This Penang the newcomers chose to ignore. More palatable was *their* Penang – an evening of fox-trots and claret and an hour or two of Spin the Bottle. This was their world, and leper colonies had no place in it. In Malaya, the British began as they meant to proceed. Though here but a few short hours, the character of their relationship with the country had already been established.

No group clung more assiduously to its ancestral ways than the British did in Malaya. The society they created so resembled the one they had left behind, its detractors called it Cheltenham on the Equator. 'The chief endeavour is to forget that the East exists,' wrote Richard Curle, the Conrad scholar. 'It is the same attitude that we adopt towards dying. But we go on dying.'

It was sheer folly, of course, this effort to deny the East's existence, but the British, past masters at allaying foreignness, were not to be deterred. A booklet published in 1915 advised intending settlers that, while riding could be indulged in all over the FMS, saddlery was not always available and should therefore be purchased in England: 'A set of stable brushes, scrapers, etc. should [also] be brought.'

The news was not so good for fishermen: 'There is very little rod fishing to be had in the federated states. Most of the rivers are polluted by the detritus washed out of the tin mines. Fishing tackle rots and goes to pieces very quickly.' A page or two later, the tone brightens. In Kuala Lumpur, we are told, 'an art association has been established for the encouragement of sketching and photography'.

There were also instructions on what clothes to bring: 'The most useful suitings are those of thin flannel and serge. A dress suit and a supply of white shirts should be taken, but neither a frock coat nor a morning coat will be required.' For headgear, the booklet recommends a pith helmet, a soft felt hat, a straw and a couple of caps. The athletic were not forgotten, either. 'If addicted to outdoor exercise,' it advised, 'the new arrival should bring white flannels, a flannel coat and half a dozen pairs of handknit knickerbocker stockings.'

Handknit knickerbocker stockings were only the half of it. In this withering equatorial heat, the British wore starched shirts or, as the *Mail* called them, 'glorified meat tins'. In the evenings, they donned tails – a survival, said the *Mail*, of 'the tortures of the Inquisition'. The possession of such a garment, the paper added, deserved to be made a penal offence. The dress code much exercised the *Mail*, a voice of reason in a country that, all too often, strikes one as deranged. Going out 'in the afternoon sun arrayed in a garb more suited to the shady side of Bond Street', made no sense, it complained, and suggested that the day was not far off when planters would be expected to inspect their trees in spats.

The British were just as uncompromising when they sat down to eat. For most, breakfast was porridge, bacon and eggs, a pot of tea and toast and marmalade. A typical dinner consisted of tomato soup, cold asparagus (served with bottled salad dressing), roast chicken (usually overcooked), mashed potatoes and tinned peas. And then there was dessert – fruit salad as often as not, also tinned.

Worthington ale and steak-and-kidney pie could be purchased at the Selangor Club where, on St George's Day, beefeaters from the Royal Society of St George, bearing heaped trays of roast beef, marched round the dining room to the strains of 'The Roast Beef of Olde England'. For the really homesick, there was Bud's Tea Room and the chance to gorge on 'creamy vanilla slices, delicious eclairs, home-made scones, toast and sandwiches and the most more-ish ices you've ever tasted'.

Once in a while, the menu at the Spotted Dog, as the Selangor Club was called, even featured bangers and mash. Curious, on the face of it. The club's members were predominantly middle-class, and many had been to public school, but nostalgia will do that. Bangers and mash had shed their plebeian associations. They no longer connoted class; now they connoted England.

In their homes, the British ate meals prepared by Chinese cooks, most of whom were ignorant of the English diet. Help, however, was available from *The Planter*, a monthly magazine published by the Incorporated Society of Planters, which often ran recipes for such staples as bread sauce, parsley stuffing, lemon tarts, angels on horseback and Welsh rarebit. At Christmas, there were instructions on how to make trifle, brandy butter and mince pies. There was even a highly ingenious recipe for strawberries and cream which dispensed with the strawberries altogether: 'A very realistic substitute can be made by thoroughly mashing up half a dozen bananas with plain Ideal milk – enough to make the mash like thick Devonshire cream. After beating this together for a few minutes, it will smell like fresh, crushed strawberries. Add two or three teaspoonfuls of strawberry jam to complete the illusion and place on ice for half an hour or so before serving.'

Just as it had criticized the dress code, the *Mail* also attacked British eating habits. This campaign also failed. The newspaper suffered a further setback when it tried to convince its readers that Malayan news was deserving of their interest. The British refused to be persuaded. One man said he was sick and tired of reading about KL. He didn't buy the *Mail* for *local* news; he brought it for news of home. Many agreed with him, and little by little, the paper yielded, running more and more items about the Derby, the test matches, Wimbledon, the FA Cup, the boat race . . .

As an editorial policy, this worked well when there were sporting events. When there weren't, the paper seems to have run whatever came to hand. In September 1909, it informed its readers: 'the vacant building sites on the Strand are at present entirely overgrown with wild flowers and grasses'. In August 1911, it reported: 'on account of the heat wave in London, the matinees of The Quaker Girl at the Adelphi Theatre have been discontinued until September.'

In the circumstances, the news in June 1911 – Mrs Proudlock would have read of this in gaol – that Francis Younghusband, the British explorer, had been injured must have seemed a godsend. June 28: 'Sir Francis Younghusband is lying in a sanitarium in Belgium with his legs fractured.' And on 5 July: 'Col. Younghusband, as a result of the recent motor car accident he met with in Belgium, has developed serious symptoms of pneumonia.' On 6 July, however, the news was better. The patient had rallied: 'A telegram from Belgium states that Sir Francis Younghusband is improving and is expected to recover.' (Though Younghusband *did* recover physically, he never recovered his faith. 'How in the face of such an experience', he asked, 'can I be expected any longer to believe in the theory that I was being looked after by a Benevolent Being?')

There was no lack of Home news on 7 May 1910. When the *Mail* appeared that day, it was bordered in black. King Edward VII had died. 'It is difficult to express in mere words', said the paper, 'the poignant and overwhelming grief which is felt by every subject of His Majesty at the terrible calamity which has befallen the empire – a calamity appalling at any time but doubly so today by reason of its suddenness. Yesterday in many lands countless thousands looked up to, revered and loved King Edward as the head of our glorious empire. Today they mourn his death.'

KL ground to a halt. Shops and offices closed. People wore black arm-bands. A cricket match was cancelled and a football match postponed. Members of the Selangor Ladies' Rifle Association called off their monthly spoon shoot. As a mark of respect, several horse-owners withdrew their entries from an upcoming race meeting. The flight of an airship was hastily rescheduled. At VI, 'the boys assembled in their various drill companies, marched up to a portrait of the late king and saluted it'. On the padang (the playing field in front of the Selangor Club) men attending a service for the dead monarch wept openly.

The British denied the East in many other ways. They played English sports, planted English gardens, read English magazines and thrilled to English music. When they painted, it wasn't to Malaya they looked for inspiration, but to Home. In January 1911, the *Mail* reviewed an art show in the VI auditorium that did not contain a single Malayan subject. Mr Crighton entered 'Kensington Gardens', Mrs Langley 'Wild Daffodils', Mr Jackson 'Westminster', and Miss Trump a series of rural sketches which, the critic said, were 'very nice in tone'.

The British so isolated themselves that they reminded Curle of the 'imprisoned aristocrats of the French revolution'. They seem not to have considered that, being abroad, they might be required to live differently; that adaptation might be in order. Instead of fashioning a new way to engage the world, they simply reproduced what they had left behind. They didn't create; they re-created. Malaya, they decided, would be a simulation of what had been sacrificed to come here. It would be a little Britain.

The institutions they had enjoyed in England were lovingly replicated: the clubs, the race courses, the bridge tournaments, the dinner parties – all those things that might delude them into thinking they were still in Sussex. (There were even old-boy dinners. Old Haileyburians, Old Bedfordians and Old Marlbarians all had branches in KL.) The British were master illusionists. Like that recipe for *faux*-strawberries, nearly everything they did in Malaya was designed to deceive.

Why do it? the *Mail* asked in 1910: 'East is east, and west is west and never the twain shall meet, yet we bring our western customs and simply dump them – that is the right word – down in an eastern land.'

There were several reasons. One was the Britons' sense of themselves as racially and culturally superior. They took great pride in what had been achieved in Malaya. In little more than a generation, it was claimed, a primitive backwater had been raised up and where once there had been anarchy, now there was order and the rule of law. The British believed that they alone could have accomplished this. The Federated Malay States, wrote the authors of *Twentieth Century Impressions of British Malaya*, provide 'the most remarkable demonstration throughout the empire of the remarkable national genius of England for colonization.

'In no part of the world is life safer or more orderly. Systematic and efficient government prevails and wealth is being amassed at a rate almost fabulous, carrying with it the introduction of the conveniences and elegance of the best civilization that the world affords.'

The British were loyal to the ways of their forebears for another reason: the Conradian notion, shared by Maugham, of the enemy within; the primitive lurking in the human heart, listening, watching, waiting for its chance to burst forth and wreak havoc. In the work of Nathaniel Hawthorne, that evil takes the form of a dark forest on the edge of every village, luring the unsuspecting. Very much the same idea animated the British. There was only one way to survive in Malaya, they believed: they had to stick together.

There could be no consorting with the Other. Do that and they risked, not just themselves, but colonialism as well – history's great effort to forge a better world. The British had not come to Malaya to assimilate. Nothing would have been more detrimental to their purpose. They were the stewards of Judgment Day, destiny's children, history's chosen instrument. *Malaya would assimilate with them.*

This was where VI came in. The school, looking like a large cottage built in the style called English Gothic, was founded in 1894 for the purpose of inculcating in Malaya's Asians England's ways and England's values. When Richard Sidney succeeded Bennett Shaw in 1922, his goal, he said, was to turn his pupils into English gentlemen. To accomplish this, Sidney, adopting as his model the English public school, established a tuck shop, divided VI into houses, created prefects and commissioned a school anthem. (It should contain lots of vowels, he told the composer, inspire *esprit de corps* and sound like the one they sang at Harrow.)

Once a year, Sidney had the prefects to dinner at his house, the bungalow the Proudlocks had lived in. (As late as 1926, first-time visitors still asked to see the bullet holes.) At seven, the prefects met on the verandah to chat and, at 7.30, sat down to dine. This is Sidney's description of one such dinner: 'The meal went along merrily. The fare was plain: oxtail soup, cold-fish jelly, roast fowl, salad, chocolate jelly, dessert and coffee. In the distance, Boy Scouts manipulated my gramophone, and strains from "Merrie England" and "The Mikado" floated through the room.' When dinner was over, the boys were offered a drink: port or *crème de menthe.* And then 'toasts were drunk . . . and after His Majesty the King Emperor, we had Ladies, Our Guests, the Prefects, etc. etc.'

Sidney's great aim, he said, was to encourage (in his pupils) 'a good speaking voice . . . Many a boy's prospects in later life would depend on how, in speaking to his future employer, he impresses that gentleman.' To improve their diction, great emphasis was placed on memorizing poetry – with mixed results. One day, Sidney visited a classroom.

'How are you getting on?' he asked the teacher, a Mr Chin.

'Very well, sir; the boys like that poetry book by Housman.'

Mr Chin then asked one of his pupils, a small Chinese boy, to recite something. The boy responded with:

> The fairies break their dances
> And leave the printed lawn
> And up from India glances
> The silver sail of Dawn.

Sidney was delighted. And then he paused. 'Do they understand much of this?' he asked Mr Chin.

'Well, sir,' said the teacher, 'they probably don't.'

Winstedt was highly critical of this kind of education. The books given Asian schoolchildren were 'bad and obscure', he complained. 'Readers contained tales of foxes and rabbits and robins . . . Arithmetic dealt with pounds, shillings and pence instead of the dollars and cents current in Malaya, while pupils who lived in palm-thatched huts and bathed in the river were set to estimate the yards of paper needed for the walls of a Victorian drawing-room and the gallons of water required to fill a bath such as they had never seen and could not conceive.'

(I visited VI in 1996, hoping to learn something about the Proudlocks, but the principal, a pleasant Malay woman, became agitated when I mentioned Steward's murder. Her assistant asked anxiously if I were a policeman.)

British children did not attend VI. They received their schooling in England. Malaya was no place for a child, the British claimed, just as once they had said it was no place for a woman. Malaya was dangerous and threatening and unpredictable. The best you could do was to keep it at a distance.

Many did not just fear Malaya; they seemed to hate it, often remarking that they could not wait to leave. In 1923, the *Mail* addressed this hostility. 'To hear [the Briton] talk, one might even imagine that he was sorry he ever came to this country, that he could do better elsewhere, and that, on the expiration of his agreement, he would have no further use for Malaya.'

Talk like this was not only unfair, it was hypocritical as well. Malaya had been good to these people. It gave them status, and it gave them wealth. Though they must have known this, they rarely acknowledged it. As late as 1938 – three years before the Japanese invasion that would make their world implode – they were still bemoaning the luck that had taken them there; still speaking of Malaya as if it were Devil's Island; still pining for that receding and ever more elusive Home.

'The call of the East is as nothing to the call of the West,' one man wrote. 'To many, the latter has never ceased to be the insistent call of their lives.' George Bilainkin, one of the few Britons actually to enjoy Malaya, felt sorry for these people. When a man left his homeland to make his name abroad, he said, he became stateless, no more a part of the country he had left than he was of the one he now resided in. He became a man of confused loyalties, a deluded man who drew nourishment from a fiction – an England so romanticized and so hopelessly embellished that, without his noticing, it had passed into myth.

7

'Kippers Always in Stock'

It is a pity that Mrs Proudlock left KL when she did, for the place had begun to liven up. In 1908, a visitor complained that the capital was all bars, rickshaws and billiard saloons, but in the three years since, KL had acquired a number of new amenities. An attractive railway station had been built, a decent hotel had opened, a cinema was in operation, the Selangor Club had grown substantially and, most important of all, Singapore Cold Storage, which specialized in meat and dairy products imported from Britain, had opened a branch not far from the Proudlocks' bungalow on High Street.

On the face of it, these additions seem modest. Yet, forty years earlier, KL had been a squalid mining village consisting of two rows of mud huts crammed into a minuscule patch of cleared jungle. Things had somewhat improved when William Proudlock arrived in 1901 but, in many ways, KL was still a primitive place. 'The streets were paved with red laterite and were illuminated by flickering kerosene lamps,' Ng Seo Buck recalled some fifty years later. 'Prisoners with chained feet and guarded by a policeman swept the streets early in the morning, and semi-nude Indian labourers did all the road repairs. In the shopping quarters, very few European ladies could be seen. When they did come out they were clad in Victorian dresses, fully veiled and gloved with their skirts trailing along the ground.'

Even then, the city of today had begun to emerge. Around the padang, once the site of a vegetable garden and a ramshackle prison, all the major institutions of British power had taken shape: St Mary's Church, an example of English Gothic; the Chartered Bank, with its curious Flemish gables; the Tudor-evoking Selangor Club; and the Secretariat. The latter, a giddy pastiche of Mogul domes and Moorish arches and owing much to British India, employed a style called neo-Saracenic. The Secretariat was to prove controversial, but not on account of its design (though it is true that many had hoped for something more Hellenic). What inspired misgivings was the building's 135-foot clock tower. Whether it was thought that the principles of engineering had been pushed to their limit or that the builder was incompetent is not clear. Whatever the reason, people feared that the gun sounded at noon every day from nearby Federal Hill (so that people could set their clocks) would destabilize it. Five minutes before mid-day, the pavement in front of the Secretariat would suddenly empty.

From the beginning, KL was a divided city. The British resided west of the Klang, and the Chinese lived on the other bank. This was no accident. The British, convinced that the Chinese meant them no good, were glad of the intervening river. It made them feel more secure. The bungalows they built occupied a line of low hills within sight of the padang and not far from the Lake Gardens, a picturesque public park boasting fountains and shaded walks, kiosks and band stands, and greensward strewn with pink and yellow petals.

The Chinese quarter, inevitably called Chinatown, straddled High Street. Lined by two-storeyed shophouses, it was KL's oldest thoroughfare and also its most frenetic. There were coffin-makers here and launderers, loan sharks and cobblers, barbers and apothecaries, tailors and pawnbrokers. On the arcaded pavements, men dipped candles and taught caged birds to sing, polished shoes and sold charms, carved jade and played mah jong. The shops were congested, too. Every inch of counter space was filled; every inch of floor. In some, there was merchandise suspended from the ceiling. Adding to all this clamour were the rickshaw pullers in their blue dungarees and peaked straw hats, always hovering, hectoring, ringing their bells, never taking no for an answer. The exhilaration of all that motion, all that self-absorbed bustle, must have been intoxicating.

At the top of High Street was the Federal Dispensary, where Ethel bought that wretched gun. ('Under no circumstances', said an ad, 'can we supply customers with cartridges unless a firearms licence is produced at the time of ordering.') Beyond the Dispensary lay the produce market, housed in a building of such gravity, people seeing it for the first time mistook it for a school or a seminary. Inside, though, it was lively and full of colour: vegetables were arranged in heaps on tables made of wooden boxes, and there were tropical fruits: rambutans (which resemble sea urchins until peeled, when what is left looks suspiciously like an eye), mangoes, jack fruit (looking for all the world like baby manatees), mangosteens, their skins a dark heliotrope, and the king of fruits, the malodorous and much-maligned durian. Bilainkin described the durian as the most abominable fruit in the world. It smelled, he said, like bad onions mixed with the contents of a sewer. And he was right. But it is also delicious. The flesh looking like a foetus, has the colour and texture of a ripe Brie.

And the taste? It reminded me of an especially delicate *crème brûlée.*

You could buy all sorts of things at the produce market. There were eggs, some with speckled shells, others with bright red yolks; slabs of meat crawling with happy flies; live crabs that wandered away when no one was watching; 'great beehive baskets from whose depths dismal quacks and cacklings' issued; objects pickled in jars, their provenance something of a mystery; and countless spices. There were shrines here, too: Buddhist ones in front of which people sat on their haunches and burned joss sticks; and others honouring the deities of India: portly gods brandishing tridents, and gods with blue faces and helmets of the type that adorned King Tut.

The British hated the place. It was too clamorous, they said, and horribly dirty. When *they* shopped, they went to Cold Storage. There was much rejoicing when the Singapore firm opened a branch in KL. The British felt their exile keenly when they sat down to table and, for years, had been forced to make do with buffalo meat, which they found unpalatable, and buffalo milk which was dangerous, since many of these animals were tubercular. Indians with a buffalo in tow were a common sight in KL; if you needed milk, you simply took a jug and went looking for one. Good bread and good pork were available locally, but few cared to eat them. The bread was made by Bengalis, and the pork raised by Chinese and, as the British were fond of putting it, 'was it worth the risk?' For some time, Cold Storage had been providing residents of Singapore with imported beef and butter. Now, those same products, along with many others, could be purchased in KL. 'English kippers always in stock,' said the advertisements. 'Ceylon tea: A new shipment has just arrived.'

The *Mail* could not have been happier. 'Six inches of snow may be seen' in the giant refrigerator, wrote one of its reporters in October 1910. 'Once the door to the chamber is opened, a mist such as seen in the Strand in November floats towards one. All around the snowy walls hang carcasses of meat, game, fish and so forth. Pheasants from the Scotch moors and salmon from Scotch streams are here hung in exile and very tempting they look, too. By means of the new machinery, installed at a cost of over $10,000, it is possible to present every kind of food and fruit to the public in the state they leave Britain.' To the relief of everyone, the expatriate table need never look foreign again.

The reaction to the cinema was equally rhapsodic. The *Mail*, indeed, could find no fault. The films were excellent, the lighting was excellent, the seating was excellent. And the pit band? That was excellent, too. Best of all was the absence of any flickering and a 'clear picture that does not tire the eyes'. It is hard not to be a little touched by the *Mail*'s enthusiasm. It seems to have embraced every one of these developments – the new station, the enlarged club, the fresh creamery butter – with the half-incredulous glee of a child opening birthday presents.

The cinema, however, KL would discover, was a mixed blessing. Those films that reflected well on the British – people being heroic, achieving great things, acting selflessly – they endorsed. Other films, ones in which the British acted badly – killing one another, stealing, committing adultery – they did not like at all. Such films gave the credulous native quite the wrong impression, the *Mail* complained, and damaged British prestige.

There was another problem, too. The cinema attracted thugs – young roughs whose idea of recreation was getting drunk and wreaking havoc. In one incident, blackguards threw lighted cigars from the balcony on to the heads of people sitting in the stalls. One woman's hair caught fire. And then they started improvising, 'hitting chairs about the hall, tossing glasses and bottles amongst the audience and obstructing the light rays of the cinematography projector'.

The *Mail* was surprisingly indulgent towards this sort of behaviour. It would be wrong, the paper said, to judge these people too harshly. They were far from home; far from a mother's restraining influence: 'So they may run a little more loose than before, those boys, but most of them run as straight as we have any right to ask or expect of them. It is not good to have it spread abroad that our young men as a whole run wild. They are just as well behaved as the young men who preceded them.'

The British liked to claim that Malaya's economic success benefited not just themselves, but the country's Asians as well. This clearly was not the case. As early as 1908, KL had an underclass. Beggars were everywhere, people complained. They were even to be found around the Spotted Dog, 'horrifying spectators by the open display of loathsome sores and deformities'. Most of these people were Chinese, but others were Indians out of work 'who drag themselves about the town, often suffering from dysentery and malaria . . . frequently in the last stages of emaciation'.

The *Mail* called on KL's sanitary board again and again to help these people. But beyond arresting beggars and putting them in the Pauper Hospital – which they promptly left because of the poor conditions – the board did nothing. In 1910, it had a more pressing concern: rats. KL, like much of the country, was overrun with them. When the planter Bruce Lockhart took his meals, rats swarmed down 'a round beam from the palm-thatched roof to the floor. My little fox terrier would then rout them out, while I stood with a rattan cane in my hand to knock the rats down as they ran up the beam again. I killed scores of them in this manner. Still better fun was shooting them with a revolver as they crawled out from the "ataps" on to the edge of the wall and sat staring at me impudently.'

The Chinese used another method: they doused rats with paraffin and set them alight. Even this failed to keep their numbers down and, in February 1911, the board was moved to act, raising the bounty on dead rodents from two cents to three. The town's health officer said the rats were a menace and accused them of spreading plague. He then issued what amounted to a call to arms, urging the public to give the rats no quarter. It was them or us, he said. If more rats were not killed, KL would face a public-health emergency.

Another problem was the telephone. Some people found it so unreliable, they chose not to use it at all, finding it less aggravating to send a letter. One man proposed getting rid of phones altogether. No telephone system, he argued, would be an improvement on the one then in existence. The electricity supply, in operation since 1907, was erratic, too. In February 1910, a second generating plant had opened, but it did not prove much of a help. Months would pass before a battery was installed.

Blackouts occurred often in KL. And they were never opportune. In February 1909, the Spotted Dog was plunged in darkness an hour before a performance of *Lady Audley's Secret* was due to start. The club, used to these emergencies, simply set out candles and resolved to press ahead. But the city was in darkness, too, and at curtain time, the audience consisted of just two people. The recital was cancelled. Lady Audley could relax; at least until the lights were restored, her secret was safe.

People fumed about the power supply and railed against the telephone, but their apoplexy they reserved for KL's laterite roads. To start with, they were potholed, the result of heavy use by bullock-carts, but worse – much worse – they produced dust, so much of it that, on occasion, movement was all but impossible. Things were especially bad in the dry season. In September 1909, the town experienced a dust storm so severe 'even the bullocks found it necessary to come to a standstill'.

The government had begun to re-metal the busier streets with durable hard roadstone, but the task proceeded slowly, largely because metal was in short supply. This was blamed on the inmates of Pudu gaol. Prisoners sentenced to hard labour were required to break metal, but many refused, reasoning that a diet of bread and water (their punishment if they did not work) was infinitely preferable to the awful drudgery of wielding a sledge-hammer in the suffocating heat.

This attitude did not sit well with Colonel R. F. S. Walker, CMG. Reporting on Malaya's prisons in September 1910, the colonel complained that, in Pudu gaol alone, more than 5,000 prisoners declined to work. Walker had his own remedy for such a flagrant breach of discipline. 'A decent flogging would stop this gross and woeful insubordination,' he said. 'Nothing else will. It is a punishment an Asiatic will respect.'

The colonel, I suspect, admired George Younghusband who, in his book *Forty Years a Soldier*, did as much as anyone to formulate the doctrine that the best Asian was a pliant Asian and, to keep him so, he should be constantly intimidated. Be civil by all means, Younghusband said, but the moment he even *hints* at insolence, 'it is wise to hit the Oriental straight between the eyes, and to keep on hitting him thus, till he appreciates exactly what he is and who he is'. This pernicious theory enjoyed wide support in Malaya and was often used to defend brutality. Because the Asian admired strength more than anything, this argument went, being nice to him availed you nothing. Indulge him at all, and you lost his respect.

The *Mail* sympathized with Colonel Walker. Just a month earlier, the paper had expressed its opposition to Winston Churchill's call to improve prison conditions, asking the question, 'Why give the habitual jailbird a bed of roses to lie on?' Alas, the colonel's hands were tied. The courts disapproved of flogging people, as the prisoners well knew. Lolling in their cells and eating their spartan rations, they could ignore Walker's diatribes. The law had placed them beyond his reach.

Metalling had now taken on some urgency because cars were making an appearance and, having done so, everybody had to have one. It is doubtful whether, in a town this size, a car was needed at all, but that hardly mattered. This was an imitative place, and those who succeeded here, whatever else they had in common, shared a talent for mimicry.

The *Mail*, whose managing director, John Robson, was an enthusiastic 'automobilist', ran a weekly feature called 'Motor Notes' in which the writer (probably Robson himself) expatiated on everything from cooling systems and dual ignitions to Gabriel horns and accumulators. The merits of the Daimler were discussed, and the shortcomings of the Fiat. And for those contemplating a motoring tour, there was advice on the best way to dress: 'The most workmanlike outfit . . . is a khaki coat and breeches with spiral putties and light boots.' A gauze singlet, short thin flannel drawers, a Burberry raincoat 'and a cap for the evenings would complete the outfit'.

It all sounds innocent enough, but read the news columns and a darker picture emerges. From the beginning, there had been complaints that cars were a nuisance: they made far too much noise and aggravated the dust problem. Now a new complaint was heard: cars were dangerous as well. They were capable of hurting people. On occasion, they could even kill.

Starting in 1910, the pages of the *Mail* began to fill with accident reports. Here are some examples from 1911: a civil servant was forced to resign when the car he was driving ran over a railway employee; Dr MacIntyre, who later that year would examine Ethel Proudlock, was badly hurt when a car rammed his rickshaw; a car struck a twelve-year-old Tamil boy, crushing his legs; and two Europeans died when their car overturned, pinning them in a drain.

There were numerous close calls, the most remarkable involving E. W. Birch, the Resident of Perak. Birch was driving in Ipoh when 'a valuable spaniel which was sitting on the seat beside him slipped as the car was rounding a bend and Mr Birch, in pulling the animal back, pulled too far and its legs got caught up with the steering wheel. The car ran into the left-hand ditch, and Mr Birch was obliged to turn the front wheels well to the right to get out. Mr Birch was badly shaken, but escaped without injury.' We are left to guess what became of the dog.

It was not easy to be a motorist. Not only were cars costly to buy and expensive to run, they were forever breaking down. Since hardly anyone knew anything about them – there were as yet few garages – very often, the owners ended up repairing them themselves. One man trusted to luck when he did this, closing his eyes and striking the engine randomly with a spanner. It worked, he said, as long as you wielded the spanner really hard.

There was another hazard: washed-out roads. Until the Klang was rerouted and its banks raised in the late 1920s, KL was prone to periodic flooding. Easily the worst occurred in 1926. For days beforehand, the flood signal had been warning the town that the river was rising and would soon break its banks. When it did, much of KL was brought to a standstill. In all, the town was under water for almost a week. Chinatown was especially hard hit. Families forced to flee their homes – some houses were completely submerged – had to forage for food and sleep rough. Several old people died of exposure. And the rats were out in force, raising the possibility of an outbreak of cholera.

The British quarter was affected, too, though not to the same extent. The padang had become a lake. (On a dare, and no doubt fortified by drink, one man swam its width – a distance of several hundred yards.) St Mary's Church was awash. The pews, refinished at some expense just a few years earlier, now bobbed in several feet of water. Not even the Chartered Bank was spared. Water seeped into the vault and saturated bank notes worth millions of dollars. Later, when the floods receded, the notes, neatly arranged in rows, were laid outdoors to dry. It was quite a sight and, naturally enough, drew the curious. People kept their distance, though, fearful perhaps of alarming the guard. A large man armed to the teeth and glowering mightily, he was the last person you would want to misconstrue your motives.

Back at VI, the flood posed problems for Richard Sidney. Not only was he running out of candles, but the rising water had begun to threaten his grand piano. To calm himself, he turned to the gramophone. '*Merrie England* soon made me forget the floods and alarms,' he wrote, 'and I played on and on until the First Act was over.' Feeling more resolute now, he sent his 'boy' into town to fetch supplies (wading across the school grounds, the servant lost his footing and nearly drowned); and then, with the help of three Chinese, he raised the piano on to several aerated-water cases. It was out of harm's way, but now he had another problem: all that exertion, he wrote, nearly broke his back.

Having returned with the candles, Sidney's 'boy' told him that 'many shopkeepers are ruined and hundreds of poor people homeless and don't know where they are going to sleep tonight'. Sidney's response was uncharacteristically selfish. Looking at his garage, he said, 'I hope my car's all right.'

When Bennett Shaw was VI's headmaster, he and his family took rooms at the Empire Hotel when the Klang broke its banks. The Empire had opened in 1909 to considerable fanfare because, while Penang and Singapore drew tourists in large numbers, KL drew hardly any. This the British blamed on the absence of decent accommodation. What the city needed, they said, was a good hotel. Now it had one. 'Fitted throughout with electrical light and supplied with electric fans', this former residence of a wealthy Chinese had been converted at great expense. Each guest had his own bathroom and 'practically all the furniture has been got from Home or from Ceylon'. The hotel, said to have the nicest lounge in KL, was also famous for its kitchen. Many looked on dinner at the Empire as something of a treat, William Steward among them. It was here he dined on 23 April 1911 before heading off for that fateful *tête-à-tête* with the vengeful Ethel.

Meals, prepared under European supervision, were elaborate. This was the menu for Thursday 20 May 1909. Tiffin: grilled fish with tartar sauce; eggs à la Milanese; salami of sheep's tongue; grilled mutton chops (to order five minutes); curried fowl; Australian mutton; smoked ham; potato croquettes; cabinet pudding; fruit and coffee. Dinner that day was even more lavish: hors d'oeuvres; tomato soup; boiled fish with butter sauce; chicken and ham pâté; filet of mutton jardinière; roast goose with apple sauce and riz l'imperatrice; cheese straws and coffee. Tiffin cost $1 and dinner $1.25.

The Empire Hotel was just one of several amenities KL could point to, said a book published in 1923. Others included a race track, a golf course, a polo ground, two clubs, prime roads, good shops, English society and a cool climate. A *cool* climate? Surely the writer was joking. And the golf course had its drawbacks, too. It was built on what had once been a Chinese cemetery which sometimes meant that golfers didn't just raise divots, they raised the dead as well, their nine-irons unearthing the skulls and bones of the long-departed.

Some of the amenities were real enough, though, so why were there not more tourists? There were two reasons: most people had never heard of KL; and, among those who had, it was considered boring. 'It is alive, it is even attractive, but it lacks personality,' Curle wrote. 'You see nothing in it of the tragic silence of history, nothing of the throes of supreme emotions. The guiding hand of a parental government hovers over all.'

KL had its opium dens and its brothels, but their patrons tended to be Chinese. Most Britons avoided such places out of caution. No one wished to offend the moralists. If an Englishman wished to consort with a prostitute, he went to Singapore. (Ever since the inauguration of a daily train service between the two cities, reaching the island had been relatively easy. The trip took twelve hours, the 'down' train leaving KL at 7.12 a.m., and the 'up' train departing Singapore at 7.05 a.m.)

Singapore was Malaya's Happy Valley, its sin capital. Bilainkin called it a miniature Paris. Here, the monasticism that ruled the rest of Malaya removed its tie and opened its collar. Unlike KL, ever priggish, Singapore did not make a fetish of human weakness. Winstedt tells of a man who attended a church service in Singapore one Sunday and how amused he had been by the choice of hymn: 'O day of sweet reflection! O day of heavenly love!' Singapore did a lot of things on Sundays, but reflecting was not one of them. It was more likely to eat a very large lunch and devote 'the afternoon to a love that the church could hardly describe as heavenly'.

In Singapore people could indulge any number of vices: gambling and sex; drugs and sex; sex and sex. 'There are plenty of houses where abominable practices are staged for the delectation of well-to-do visitors,' said Bilainkin, mercifully refraining from going into detail. But most sex was the mundane sort: encounters with other men's wives, or encounters with other men, encounters with members of other races. In Singapore, people got up to all kinds of mischief. One man left his family to live with a Chinese heiress. (His wife and children became the responsibility of a jockey from Australia.) Another was discovered to be married to three women all at once. And a third was shot in the rump by an irate husband who found him in bed with his wife. This was unusual; most cuckolds took their revenge by making someone else a cuckold. Singapore winked at all of this. At times, it seems to have looked benignly on everything – monogamy being the big exception.

Naturally, those going to the island in search of pleasure would never admit as much. Press them, and they would say that their reasons were professional: a client was visiting for a day or two; or a contract needed signing. In time, these evasions became something of a joke. Men heading south to close a spurious deal or to confer with a non-existent partner were referred to as the urgent-business brigade.

Singapore had many advantages for the man seeking gratification, but easily the most important was its distance from KL. Little chance of discovery here. The city was a busy port and full of foreigners. A man could do as he pleased and attract no notice. It helped also that Singapore was largely Chinese. (Some spoke of it as China's nineteenth province.) The British felt constrained around Malays who, bound as they were to Islam, tended to be censorious. The Chinese were another matter. No hard and fast rules for them. Their morality was a relative one, and its effect was to make them non-judgmental.

Singapore, being Chinese, had another advantage: not liking the Chinese very much, the British did not feel compelled to court their good opinion. While they hesitated to scandalize the Malays, going to elaborate lengths to protect their sensibilities, around the Chinese niceties were forgotten.

Not everyone who went to Singapore did so to wallow in vice. Some were drawn by curiosity. When Winstedt and two fellow cadets visited the red-light district in 1902, their first stop was a music hall called the Tingle-Tangle. Providing the entertainment that night was 'a chorus of fat, white Austrian girls, dressed in the scarlet and green and white of the Tyrol and looking as if they would like to yodel, if the dank heat would not turn that exercise into a gargle'. From there, they went to a brothel on Malay Street – Winstedt must have been sober; he remembers it having green shutters – where 'like orchids in a conservatory, Japanese ladies sat behind bamboo bars with paper flower-garlands on their heads, too utterly doll-like to excite desire'. No coitus that night. After an hour of drinking warm beer and speaking pidgin English, all three men returned to their hotel. 'Nurtured . . . in Kipling imperialism, we were not sure if curiosity excused "stewards of the Judgement Day" from visiting such a house,' Winstedt wrote later, 'but we quieted our conscience with the thought that Kipling would have accompanied us and that we had promoted international friendship.'

Windstedt was a rare exception. Most of those who came to Singapore, whether they meant to or not, ended up indulging themselves. Even Maugham found it irresistible. While here, he smoked opium and had a dream: he was on a road of the sort 'that you see often in France, and it stretched in front of me, white and straight, immensely far; I saw farther than I had ever thought it possible to see, and still the white road continued with green poplars on either side. And then . . .

the poplars flew past me more quickly, infinitely more quickly than the telegraph poles fly past when you are in an express train. Then . . . there were no poplars . . . and presently I came upon an open space and then, as I looked down, far below me, was the grey calm sea.'

He woke next morning with a throbbing headache and cursed his lack of discipline. He never smoked opium again.

8

Miss Aero and the Inimitable Denny

The new cinema aside, the British had few options when it came to amusing themselves. People complained that KL's social life lacked variety. 'Life here consists of drinking and bridge,' a man said in 1909. Many people had started to tire of both. In a letter to the *Mail* in April that year, 'Anxious Flapper' suggested that ladies attending the dance on Empire Day wear masks. 'It would', she predicted, 'tend to make things more animated.'

Something more than masks was needed. In March 1909, the *Mail* published this list of upcoming events:

March 22: Choral Society. Full Rehearsal.
March 27: Cricket: Lake Club v. The Rest.
March 28: Rifle Club Spoon Shoot.
March 29: Choral Society practice. Ladies only.
April 3: Cricket: Selangor v. Recreation Club.
April 5: Choral Society practice.
April 8: Choral Society practice.
April 9–15: Selangor Golf Club annual prize meeting.
April 10: Cricket: Selangor v. Singapore.

Let's face it; it makes for less than exciting reading.

There were bright spots, one of which was the dance every Saturday in the Spotted Dog. The event drew quite a crowd. In addition to civil servants (known for being stodgy) and their wives (even stodgier), planters attended in large numbers, though in some cases it entailed driving up to sixty miles. For most, it was worth it. Life on the more remote estates could be horribly lonely. On Saturdays, for the first time in almost a week, they could consort with others of their kind.

Dances were held in the larger of the club's two reading rooms where, early on Saturday, the magazine racks were removed and the carpets taken up. Then began the process of 'treating' the floor. First, one crew of 'boys' sprinkled the surface with powdered chalk, and then a second crew took over, jumping up and down with varying degrees of vigour until the chalk had been absorbed. A powdered floor gives dancers traction. The last thing anyone wanted was to slip and break a leg.

Despite the precautions, these dances, and others like them, often turned out to be joyless affairs. Harry Foster, an American journalist, described a dance he attended in Singapore: 'At the wicker tables upon the wide verandah sat men and women in evening dress; an English orchestra was trying to play ragtime, and couples were dancing stiffly in the British fashion, seemingly with little enjoyment, as though merely performing a rite required by society.'

The British were not exuberant dancers. In the Spotted Dog, the Selangor State Band, its programme chosen by William Proudlock, largely confined itself to foxtrots and waltzes. More exotic fare, such as the tango and the samba, was studiously avoided, the British taking the view that any music that required them to lower their dignity was inherently subversive.

There was another reason for steering clear of the samba: in Malaya's withering heat, strenuous exertion was avoided as much as possible. True, Brazil was quite as torrid and people there danced the samba to no ill effect, but in Brazil, sensible people did not as a matter of course wear ball gowns or take to the floor in tails. The British did. The proper dress on these occasions included not just cummerbunds and waistcoats, but starched collars as well which, needless to say, did not stay starched for long. Some men brought along several spares, changing collars as often as three or four times a night. And always to no avail. When the band struck up the national anthem, they were so wet through, they looked as if they had fallen in the Klang.

The heat created problems for women as well. It is the aim of every woman 'to maintain a dainty and fresh appearance throughout a dance', said the *Mail*, 'since to become heated and flushed is detrimental to beauty, besides being uncomfortable.' Well, yes. But women *did* become heated, and there was little they could do about it. Not so, said the *Mail*. 'By taking a few simple precautionary measures when dressing, it is possible to ensure that one shall look one's best during the evening.' Don't drink hot coffee, the paper advised, and on no account steam the face. (For some reason, plum puddings and double-boilers come to mind.) Instead, the visage 'should be wiped over with a very weak lotion containing one part of borax to about three parts of water'.

Over time, the number of women attending dances declined. It is hard to say why: a reluctance to use borax, perhaps; or an inability to forswear coffee. (In an effort to lure the ladies back, the Spotted Dog, at one point, offered to admit them free of charge.) Or then again, the men may have been to blame. There were altogether too many of them.

In the early 1900s, they outnumbered females three to one, with the result that women, reluctant to refuse a man in case he take offence, found themselves dancing even when they did not care to. This might not have mattered had their partners any skill, but KL seems to have lacked a Ravinsky, the planter in *Rubber*, Madelon Lulofs' novel about the Dutch East Indies. (His 'feet moved obediently to the rhythm of the music'; he 'danced for the sake of the dance', forgetting everything around him; he was 'elegant, smartly dressed ... executing the newest dance steps with perfect poise'; he was 'the ideal partner – sensing at once the essence of [a woman's] style of dancing, and adapting himself to it'.) One woman complained that every time she attended a dance in the Spotted Dog, she spent Sunday taking foot-baths and Monday buying replacement shoes.

Those men who did not care to dance or were too shy to try congregated on the verandah and looked sheepish until, feeling that they had done all that could reasonably be expected of them, they repaired to the bar and got very drunk. British Malaya was lenient in its view of heavy drinkers. It wasn't their fault, people said; the culprit was the East. Malaya drove men to alcohol, even abstemious men; men who, in England, had imbibed nothing more compromising than a glass of port once in a while or an occasional pre-prandial sherry.

People drank because they were bored, because they were lonely, or because they lacked for things to do. They drank as well because drink was cheap. In 1908, a bottle of gin cost 90 cents and a bottle of good scotch a little more than a dollar. Beer was inexpensive, too. For $3.75, you could purchase eight dozen lagers. 'With things so cheap,' C. R. Harrison wrote in *The Planter*, 'it was not surprising that drink was absorbed in enormous quantities with a consequent loss to Malaya of many valuable and able men who shortened their lives and damaged their careers.'

Food prices increased during the early part of the twentieth century as did the cost of housing, though neither seems to have generated any great concern. But when drink prices rose, however slightly, the outcry was immediate, and it was fierce. In April 1909, the *Mail* accused the Town Hall of cheating its patrons after one man complained of having to pay $1.20 for three brandy-sodas. 'No one grudges the contractor a profit,' the paper said, 'but when one considers that during race meetings the contractor supplies all ordinary drinks at 25 cents each, the above prices appear exorbitant.'

Yet even the *Mail* admitted that the British drank far more than was good for them. Even allowing for the fact that everyone enjoys a stimulant once in a while, 'it is still amazing what we all put away'. On the weekends, some people were known to drink cocktails with breakfast, slings all morning, *stengahs* with tiffin, refreshers after lunch and *pahits* at the club, by which time it was seven o'clock, the magic hour, when no pretext was needed. Now they could drink to their hearts' content. And many did. 'It is legitimate, customary and sociable to go on drinking until 8.30 or 9 when the aperitif before dinner must be consumed,' said the *Mail*. 'Dinner is a repetition of lunch plus sherry, and perhaps claret . . . After dinner, we linger over liqueurs of all shades. At 10 o'clock, we are thirsty again, and when that thirst is quenched and we seek our beds, behold a bedside tray containing a goodly array of bottles to be partaken of if we awake in the night.'

People would not drink so much, it was argued, were KL less of a cultural backwater. How romantic this sounds: people guzzling gin night in, night out because they were not getting sufficient Bach. But this does not accord with the facts. This was a low-brow crowd. On those occasions when touring artists did come to town – tenors, sopranos, the occasional pianist – they played to near-empty houses. Even the great Pavlova could not stir their interest. In December 1922, the *Mail* announced with some excitement that the dancer would perform a programme of her signature pieces at the Coliseum. 'Those who have seen her in London will never forget her,' the paper said and advised its readers to purchase their tickets quickly or risk being disappointed.

On 19 December, the performance was cancelled. The dancer was exhausted, said a bulletin, and had been told by her doctor to rest. This was a little odd because, just a day later, Pavlova performed in Singapore and showed no signs of tiredness at all. Quite the contrary. According to one critic, he had never seen her in better form. Clearly, the claim that she was indisposed was a face-saving measure. The celebrated dancer had cancelled because tickets were not selling.

British preferences did not extend to *bel canto* any more than they did to ballet. Bilainkin dreaded going to the opera, not because the singing was mediocre, but because the audience behaved so badly. The British gave every impression of being bored stiff: they arrived late, yawned, fidgeted, were for ever changing seats – in short, they made a general nuisance of themselves. When act one ended, there was a stampede for the bar. (One man likened it to Pamplona when the bulls were running.) The intention now was to fortify oneself for the rigours that lay ahead. Act two loomed ('A double scotch, waiter'). And after it, acts three and four ('Make that *two* double scotches'). By the end of the evening, some in the audience were slumped in their seats and snoring loudly.

Will Proudlock knew as well as anyone how philistine the British were. As a member of the choral society, he worked valiantly to encourage an interest in *Lieder*, but the society's following was minuscule. In August 1909, it performed in the

Town Hall to what was almost an empty house. (Or, as the always orotund *Mail* put it, the audience was 'small indeed in numbers'.) The society tried again six months later, though hardly with better results. The audience was again small – about 100 people, the *Mail* estimated. Even worse: it was not in a mood to be taxed. When Proudlock and another man performed a programme of two-part songs, the coughing and shifting reached such a pitch that the singers were barely audible. 'The Long Day Closes was well rendered,' the *Mail* sniffed next day, 'but Simple Simon was perhaps more suited to the audience.'

More to English tastes were smoking concerts (a kind of stag party which women were barred from attending) and vaudeville. They loved vaudeville. When a touring company called The Merrymakers played KL in November 1908, the engagement was a sell-out. 'A combination of artists presenting a refined musical entertainment,' said an advertisement. 'Including Zeno, the marvellous equilibrist; novelty dancers and singers; English comedy sketch artists, and Reg Williams, comedian and eccentric dancer.'

The *Mail* pronounced it brilliant. 'The company is obviously a first-rate one,' it said. 'Two or three of Zeno's conjuring tricks were as clever as anything we have seen. One of these is worth mentioning in detail. The performer takes a billiard cue, balances it on his nose, makes it turn a somersault and balances it again on his head.' The paper also singled out for praise 'the comedians Messrs Lydon and Williams'. The latter was especially funny, despite being 'handicapped by a broken wrist', sustained, one supposes, during one of his eccentric dances. The Merrymakers became the most successful company of its kind ever to visit KL.

In August 1910, the British turned out in large numbers to see Harmston's Circus. Even the acting Resident-General was there. Or, to quote the *Mail*, he graced the proceedings with his presence. KL was very much a circus town, and Harmston's did well there, announcing later that, though it had been touring the East for over two decades, its take in KL set an all-time record.

The year 1910 was a busy one. September saw the appearance – his first in the FMS – of the inimitable Denny, master of mysteries. Denny, ably assisted by Miss Aero, gave 'interesting and mystifying illustrations in necromancy and demonology', said the *Mail*. He also caused 'canaries, ducks and pigeons to appear and disappear in a truly mysterious fashion. The Asiatic audience especially appeared to be much impressed.' Though by the sound of it, not nearly as much as the *Mail* was.

Picnics were another popular diversion. And they tended to be elaborate. Not for these people a cloth spread under a tree, a bottle of wine and a couple of sandwiches; they ate *al fresco* much as they did indoors: seated on real chairs at a real table laid with the best china, the best glass and the best silver. In August 1910, the *Mail* carried a report of what it called a record picnic: 'A great picnic party of about 36 persons visited the Crag Hotel on Penang Hill yesterday. A record number of coolies – 189 – was engaged. The function was a great success.' Visiting Penang Hill in 1996, I saw a photograph of another picnic, this one from 1912: four men are seated around a table piled high with empty plates. From the look of things, they have just that minute polished off a considerable meal, and, very soon now, indigestion will strike. But for the moment, cigars in hand, they are content. They look very smug, the four of them, with their William Morris beards and their swelling bellies. In the background, five small figures huddle – their servants, presumably – eyeing the quartet with obvious apprehension.

Another entertainment much in vogue was the fancy-dress ball. One in Seremban in September 1909 was deemed to be a particular success, not least for the fact that there were a lot of women present. 'The floor was absolutely perfect,' the *Mail* enthused, 'and everything went well from start to finish.' The costumes on view that night included a laundry maid, a grass widow, a gypsy, a Turk, a waiter, a blind man, an Italian musician (replete with monkey), and a mad hatter. At another ball three months later – this one in KL – there was another Turk, another maid and, this time, *three* gypsies: a common-or-garden gypsy, a poor gypsy and a Spanish gypsy.

The British also went to the club, of course, and talked what the journalist G. L. Peet called 'colonial shop'. People said nothing of substance, he claimed. They talked for the sake of talking and because 'they would feel uncomfortable if they sat silent and stared at each other'. The *Mail* agreed. The Spotted Dog had its virtues, but the paper doubted 'if the interpretation of symphonies is discussed (there) or the theory of evolution debated'. People were stagnating, the *Mail* warned, and something should be done to stem the rot. The *Mail*'s suggestion? A debating society. 'Few of the newcomers in Malaya can afford a piano or have the energy to read deeply. Thus would a debating society be of infinite use.' But others did not agree. They went to the club for peace and quiet, people said; not to listen to a lot of self-important windbags. The proposal was quietly dropped.

Were it not for its clubs, there would have been little social life in British Malaya. There were clubs for everything: football, tennis, hockey, golf, cricket, rowing, polo, swimming, gardening. Most intriguing of all was the hunt club. When first mooted, it raised eyebrows. Where, people wanted to know, were the hounds to come from? Hounds were introduced to Malaya again and again, but the climate – along with such predators as panthers and tigers – almost always proved too much for them. Some hounds must have survived because, for a time in the 1890s, the Selangor pack hunted regularly. 'Deer and pig were often bagged and invariably an enjoyable few hours were put in,' wrote 'Kimba' in *Bygone Selangor*, 'but somehow owing to lack of support and enthusiasm the pack dwindled down.' In one pack, as many as twenty-four dogs died, their deaths attributed to 'various causes'. How hypocritical this seems. The British, who were ever accusing the Chinese of abusing animals, could at times be just as callous.

Penang also had a hunt club – this one mounted – though on the evidence it fared little better. During a paper chase in 1910, 'one horse was brought down by a barbed wire maliciously nailed up across a gap in a bamboo hedge after the paper had been laid. A mishap also occurred through a wooden bridge across a stream giving way, Miss Mahler and her horse being thrown into the sand and water below. Neither was injured. The paper chase finished at Crosby Hall where Mr P. P. Henson, assistant superintendent of police, dislocated his shoulder while dancing and had to be taken to hospital.' A bad day all round, it would appear.

Clubs were not without their critics. Some complained that by withdrawing into places like the Spotted Dog, by consorting only with one another, the British had turned their backs on Malaya. Others defended the clubs, arguing that they provided respite. Around Asians, these people contended, the British were required to be exemplary. At the club, surrounded by their own kind, they could let their guard down and be themselves. This was nonsense. The British were never more guarded than when around their countrymen. Commit a *faux pas* in the presence of a Chinese and he was unlikely to notice, but put a foot wrong at the club, make even one false move,

William Steward on the steps of what was probably his house in Salak South.

William Proudlock (second row, centre) with members of VI's First Eleven.

People on the padang watching a football game, 1903.

Kuala Lumpur during the floods of 1902.

The Victoria Institution – the school at which William Proudlock was acting headmaster.

The British go to the races.

Ladies' Day at the Swimming Club.

Salak South, the mine at which William Steward worked.

Members of the Perak Ladies' Rifle Association. Ethel Proudlock belonged to a similar club in Selangor.

Kuala Lumpur's grandiose railway station.

Members of the Penang Amateur Dramatic Society. Ethel Proudlock, another aspiring actress, trod the boards in Kuala Lumpur.

The Federal Dispensary, where Ethel bought the murder weapon. The figure in the oval inset is F.V. Guy, nemesis of the Weld's Hill monkey.

Houses in KL's Chinatown (not far from the Proudlock's bungalow).

A tiger hunt. Ethel's father was a keen hunter.

The home of a district officer.

Labourers tap rubber trees.

A house an estate manager might have lived in.

The residency where the Proudlocks celebrated the king's birthday.

and there was no telling the consequences. You were marked now as someone who didn't measure up, someone who was wanting. Yes, you could still go to the Spotted Dog, but your reception was cooler, and people were not as quick to buy you drinks. And then you noticed that the invitations had started to slow. Not surprisingly, most people chose to play it safe.

By 1910, the Selangor Club had evolved from a small wooden structure with a straw roof to a large central building flanked by wings and designed to look like the black-and-white timbered houses of Elizabethan England. The club now had a bar, two reading areas, a restaurant and numerous rooms, some for changing, some for billiards, some for playing cards. It had more than a thousand members, many of whom lived outside KL, and was seen by many as an important amenity. But not everyone was enamoured of the place. Richard Sidney went there as little as he could. He was shy and did not like to drink. This was a big failing in British eyes. The man who avoided alcohol was thought to have something wrong with him. Or worse, he was considered pretentious. 'People will be apt to say that you are aloof and proud,' Sidney was warned, 'and they will entirely misjudge the reason for your absence.' Sidney conceded that he ought to visit the club occasionally, 'if only to hear current scandal'.

All this club-hopping, all this drinking was expensive. Or it would have been had anyone actually paid for it. Most people charged. They had an account at the club, an account at the hotel, an account at the department store, and an account at Cold Storage. When they made a purchase, they signed a chit. The chit system was almost universal in the early days – the period up to 1910. At one time it even extended to church collections. It had its drawbacks, though. People were encouraged to live beyond their means, running up bills so large they could no longer pay them, while the firms and institutions extending this credit found themselves so strapped for cash, many were driven to near-bankruptcy. In January 1910, the Empire Hotel ran this advertisement in the *Mail*: 'We beg to point out that the terms of the hotel are strictly cash. Visitors residing at the hotel are required to pay their accounts when leaving. Casual visitors for meals are required to pay the chits they have signed immediately on presentation.' The Empire was not acting capriciously; because of bad debts, it had finished its first year of business considerably in the red.

Even the *Mail* admitted that the chit had become an anachronism. 'In the old days,' it editorialized in January 1911, 'the argument most frequently heard in favour of the [chit] system was that the coins of the East were too bulky to carry about with comfort – especially with white clothing. But nowadays when bank notes are generally and increasingly used this useful argument has lost much of its force.'

It had always been KL's ambition if not to emulate Singapore, at least to rival it. That never happened. Dull in 1910, KL became ever duller. If, in the Proudlock years, people complained that the town had no social life to speak of, two decades later, they had changed their minds, claiming that the social scene was now contrived. The British had become self-conscious, said the *Mail*: 'They think about precedence, their position, their clothes, their means and what other people think. Heavens! How seldom does it matter what other people think. Wherever society gathers in any sort of crowd, there is a reserve like an enveloping mist. People are afraid to be natural and human except round the bar or in their own houses.'

Starting around 1910 and extending into the 1930s, Malaya became increasingly puritanical. A man might still consort with an Asian woman, but he was more careful now and would never risk being seen with her in public. There were calls as well for additional censorship. When Maugham's play *Rain* was staged in KL in 1927, one man said he left the theatre feeling 'besmirched with filth'. (*Rain* tells the story of an American missionary who falls in love with a prostitute.) Clubs came in for renewed attack, not because of the wedge they drove between the races but because they were said to be frivolous. There was more to life than drinking and playing bridge, said the moralists. People were neglecting their families; their place was in the home. Some suggested closing clubs, if not completely, then at least for several nights a week. This did not happen, of course, for moralists lacked numbers. But whereas two decades earlier, efforts like this would have been derided, now, in the 1930s, they were taken seriously.

Why had attitudes altered so much? A generational change had occurred. In the early days – the period before 1900 – the British had had fun in Malaya. The pioneers, it was true, had not been averse to making money but they were fired as well by a spirit of adventure. Growing up, many had devoured the books of G. A. Henty: *With Clive in India, With Kitchener in Soudan, The Bravest of the Brave, Facing Death, Gallant Deeds, In the Hands of the Malays* and dozens of others. (*In the Hands of the Malays* is wooden even by Henty's standards. 'If we are successful,' says Van Houten, 'we shall at one blow destroy the power of this terrible pirate, the Sea Tiger, and render the sea open again to commerce. They will be here in an hour's time, and we'll give the Malays a reception that they do not dream of. The lesson will be so terrible that it will be a long time before any other is likely to follow the Sea Tiger's example.' But the climactic battle is stirring enough: 'With loud yells, the Malays rushed forward . . . drawing their krises . . .' The twelve-year-old who failed to find *that* exciting had ice in his veins.).

By 1920, the pioneering spirit was all but extinguished. The newer immigrants had not come to seek adventure; they were there to advance themselves, and the result was a deadening conformity. KL had become more rigid, more exclusive. People were being held to a higher standard. While some deplored this change, there was no reversing it. In the old days, one man wrote, life was freer, simpler, less conventional, not at all like 'the imported London suburb atmosphere that prevails today'.

That non-conformists were losing ground was evident as early as 1911 when the Spotted Dog announced a crackdown on what it called 'undesirables'. The club defined as an undesirable anyone whose behaviour it considered 'inappropriate'. This was intentionally vague. The club wanted at its disposal a mechanism with which it might expel for whatever reason those it didn't like. People had little choice now. Either they conformed or they became outcasts.

Significantly, the crackdown occurred one month after Steward's murder and five months after the death of F. V. Guy. When Guy died, mauled by a panther in December 1910, an era ended. He was the last of Malaya's 'characters', a genuine eccentric who accepted no authority but his own. Educated at Uppingham and a fellow of the Royal Meteorological Society, he owned his own zoo, said to contain the finest collection of animals, birds and reptiles in the FMS. It included two orang-utans each of whom liked liquor and who, at day's end, joined Guy for a *stengah.* They made, he said, amiable drinking companions.

When Harmston's Circus visited KL just four months before he died, Guy announced his intention to enter the animal cages and frolic with the tigers. He was livid when the authorities withheld their permission. Their objection, he said, 'is all very well when directed in the right direction, but when it is misdirected and interferes with the liberty of action of a British subject it is intolerable'.

A bald man with fine features and a massive moustache, he was nominally in charge of the Federal Dispensary, the store in which Ethel Proudlock bought Will his birthday present. I say 'nominally' because Guy was easily distracted. In November 1908, for example, he spent several weeks hunting down the Weld's Hill monkey. In the space of a month and a half, the monkey had attacked five people, one of them a Malay who described the animal to police as a monstrous thing with a fringe of hair encircling its face.

Guy decided it was time for action. Assembling a posse and a pack of hounds, he set out on 6 November armed to the teeth. The monkey eluded him. Next day, he was out again, spending in all twelve hours in the jungle, during which he bagged one porcupine, one wild dog and *two* monkeys, neither of which, sad to say, was the miscreant.

On the 8th, the monkey struck again, this time attacking a Chinese boy who was wounded in three places 'and was taken to hospital bleeding profusely'. By now, Guy had bagged eleven monkeys and was becoming impatient, but three days later, it was all over. 'The Weld's Hill monkey is no more,' the *Mail* reported. In the event, it was not Guy who dispatched the offending animal, but one of his party, a young Dyak. But credit, the *Mail* insisted, rightly belonged to Guy, 'who has been unremitting in his endeavours to rid the locality of the pest'.

Guy was magnanimous in victory. With much ceremony, the monkey was brought in a rickshaw to KL's natural history museum ('the only rickshaw ride that had ever fallen to his lot') where the animal was stuffed and given his own display case, the *Mail* predicting that, 'in years to come, he will doubtless be able to continue his triumphal career by striking terror into the hearts of refractory children'. There is a sense of play here, a spirit of fun, that would disappear when Guy passed away at the age of thirty-eight. His death was horrible. In addition to being mauled, part of his leg had been shot away. According to the *Mail*, he made light of his problems: 'Guy remained bright and cheerful to the end which occurred about 26 hours after the accident.'

Guy was also famous for his exertions on Empire Day. In 1909, he built a replica of a dreadnought that so impressed the Earl of Meath that His Lordship sent him an autographed photograph and a letter expressing his congratulations. The replica, over 40 feet long and constructed around Guy's car, does sound spectacular. 'The idea of a ship under her own steam was very realistic,' said the *Mail*, 'especially as smoke was constantly pouring from the funnels. It was built up forward with two tripod masts and two squat funnels painted the correct dull grey of the navy. It was literally bristling with guns.'

It was a day KL would long remember. Making it even more memorable was the speech a senior British official gave that afternoon in which he enjoined an audience of several hundred schoolboys to remember the words of Nelson: England expects that every man will do his duty. 'The empire requires self-sacrifice,' he went on. 'As the imperial government has protected us with its fleets and its armies, the time is coming when the daughter nations must do their share for the sympathy and defence the mother country has given them.'

Empire Day loomed large in Malaya's social calendar, but even more important was the king's birthday, an occasion marked by a ball at Carcosa, the home of the resident-general. The Proudlocks did not attend the ball in November 1908. Mrs Proudlock had returned from England with her baby daughter just two days earlier and the journey, no doubt, would have left her fatigued.

They did turn out for the 1909 ball which, according to the *Mail*, was a great success: 'Carcosa was prettily decorated for the occasion. [The floral] arrangements were excellent. The dance floor was in perfect order and was made full use of by a large number of guests. For the non-dancers, there were cards and other attractions.'

The ball two years later – this time on 3 June when a new king, George V, was on the throne – was spectacular, said the *Mail*: 'A special feature of the illuminations was the crown of red, green and pale yellow electric lamps on the big gable over the porch which made the terrace quite brilliant and shed a light which must have been visible for a great distance.'

Mrs Proudlock wasn't among the guests that evening. She was in Pudu gaol, still awaiting trial and wearing not her long green tea gown but prison clothes. Perhaps from her tiny cell with its wooden bed and wooden pillow, she was able to see those coloured lamps. She would, of course, have known about the ball; known that, just two miles away, others danced under Chinese lanterns as she had danced but two years earlier. It must have been a long, long night.

9

The Queen in her Garden

To see the British *en famille*, people said, was to see them at their best. Writing letters on their verandahs or playing Ludo in their parlours, they underwent a transformation. All pretence gone now – there being no one around to impress – they became themselves again: decent people, gracious people, the people they had been when they lived in England. In point of fact, however, the British within were as autocratic as they were without, ruling their households as imperiously as the fifth-form boys ruled Rugby in *Tom Brown's Schooldays*.

Like most, Richard Sidney's household was run by a head 'boy' whose talents ran the gamut. In addition to being his personal attendant, he ironed Sidney's clothes, darned his frayed shirts, ran errands and, in his spare time, of which he cannot have had very much, drove his employer's car. Sidney – this was a household of one, remember – also employed a cook, and a second 'boy', 'whose duty is that of general servant about the house'. By Malayan standards, Sidney's home was lightly staffed. The more typical British household had as many as eight servants: a head 'boy', a cook, a driver, a water carrier, a gardener, a dhoby, a nanny and a person whose job it was to clean.

In Malaya, Bilainkin said, men 'have but to shave themselves and eat. Everything else is done for them.' That way lies degeneracy. Nothing corrupts a man more quickly than being waited on. Once so self-reliant, the British became infants again, looking to servants, not only to cook and clean, but to help them into their shoes and to knot their ties – things that, in England, they'd have done reflexively. Sidney acknowledged as much when, speaking about his head 'boy', he said, 'I should find it very difficult to dress without him now!'

Very quickly, servants were taken for granted. It was only when a lapse occurred – the morning tea was late or the paper had been folded badly – that anyone paid them any notice. Rarer still were those moments when a servant who shared a roof with you and who crossed your path many times a day did or said something that made you realize that here was a being with desires and passions much like your own.

In the case of G. L. Peet, the author of *Malayan Exile*, that epiphany occurred the day the family terrier died. The Peets missed their dog, though not nearly as much as the 'boy' did. The man was inconsolable, and Peet was astonished. Until now, he'd never much thought about his servants. Who would have imagined they could feel so deeply? The experience, though, taught him little. He wrote later that though his cook had worked for him for years, it had never occurred to him to inquire as to his name. And something else: when Peet got home in the evenings, his Tamil gardener made a laughable show of obeisance, hurling down his scythe and whipping off his hat before leaping to attention. Peet said it always made him feel like an aristocrat before the revolution, yet there is no suggestion that it made him uncomfortable. Though he never actually says so, Peet, I suspect, found it gratifying.

As much as they depended on their servants, the British do not seem to have liked them very much. When the mems got together, Bilainkin tells us, servants were all they talked about – and they were rarely complimentary. Words like 'thick' and 'stupid' and 'indolent' were bandied about; phrases like 'blue in the face' and 'driven to distraction' and 'talking to the wall'. The mems also liked to say that their servants couldn't cook. Given that most servants hailed from China, a country that had produced one of the world's great cuisines, and that the British had a comparatively poor culinary tradition, this seems a bit rich.

This is not to say that Chinese cooks did not err once in a while, but even then, their problems owed more to inexperience than to any lack of skill. When Winstedt was in hospital with malaria, one of his nurses was given a Christmas pudding which she sent to 'the mess cook thinking he would know what to do with it'. The cook served the pudding 'in soup plates heavily diluted with gravy'. Some years earlier, a cook employed by the Spotted Dog had done something even more heinous: handed a haggis, he cut it into small pieces and made sandwiches of it.

While 'cookie' was the chief villain in Malaya's demonology, the dhoby or washerman came a close runner-up. The dhoby, sometimes Chinese but more often Indian, hardly deserved the odium in which he was held. He worked hard – and for very little. But the calumnies persisted. He was likened to Tamerlaine and was accused of bringing 'the art of destroying clothes to a far higher pitch of perfection than has the most up-to-date steam laundry in England'.

The dhoby's 'objectionable practices' did not bear dwelling on, the *Mail* said in 1910, but this at least was clear: he would never understand western notions of hygiene. He piled clean clothes on top of dirty clothes, 'a fruitful method of transmitting disease'. Even worse, the dhoby was a natural democrat, placing in one large heap 'all sorts and conditions of dirty linen belonging to every class of people'. That was the crux of it: the idea that one's shirt – a garment that a night earlier had sported 'our most valued diamond solitaire', as one dandy put it – might actually rub shoulders with the linens, if they could be called that, of a man who laboured for a living; linens that had graced the back of a Chinese or an Indian. It was this the British found repellent. Asians were dirty and disease-ridden. Even contact at two or three removes could lead to trouble.

Servants were also accused of being dishonest: the driver stole petrol from the car, the 'boy' food from the kitchen, and the gardener greens from the lettuce patch. The nanny drank milk intended for the baby, the dhoby made off with one's best socks, and 'cookie' added 10 per cent to everything he purchased. Even if true, it does seem petty. These people were paid a pittance, after all. And it is not as though the British, with their ceaseless hectoring and their endless calling to account, inspired much loyalty.

Far from being dishonest, servants over all were models of probity. When Indian troops mutinied in Singapore in 1915, many British families had to flee their homes. Some were in hiding for nearly a week – plenty of time for a servant, if that were his goal, to rob them blind. Yet nothing was touched. 'The servants of many nationalities – Indian, Malay, Chinese, Javanese, etc. – were marvellous,' one woman wrote afterwards. 'They had our houses all to themselves . . . so that we were completely at their mercy. Yet not a single case of theft on their part was reported to the police.'

This is not to suggest that all servants were paragons; some could be very trying. Returning home one night, Winstedt was startled to find that his 'temporary waiter . . . had set as a fern-pot in the middle of the dining-table one of those vessels . . . which European modesty used to keep under the bed and which European science has now abolished from better-class houses.' From better-class houses, maybe; not from sultans' palaces. Visiting one of Malaya's hereditary rulers a month later, Winstedt saw something that stopped him in his tracks. There on the sultan's sideboard, and displayed with obvious pride, was not just one *pot de chambre,* but two. (Winstedt never actually uses the term 'chamber pot'. Unfailingly delicate, he refers to it as an 'obscene vessel'.)

If the British did not like their servants very much, their servants did not like them, either. They ran away in droves. The British, in such cases, turned to the courts. A warrant was sought, a search was begun, the fugitive found and returned to his master – even if that master had been abusing him. Any wages he was owed were confiscated, and a fine was levied after which the magistrate would issue a warning: run away again, and the servant would find himself in gaol.

With few alternatives at their disposal, some servants, goaded beyond endurance, assaulted their employers. And there were others, though their numbers are few, who resorted to murder. Though the reasons are not known and the perpetrator was never brought to book, a former servant is believed to have killed Mr and Mrs Charlton Maxwell. Maxwell, married to a Malay, was until he retired a distinguished civil servant. Those he worked with described him as a difficult man who frequently lost his temper. The Maxwells were gunned down in their home in 1940, he while he slept, she while attempting to hide in a cupboard. Their killer, whose rage seems to have been boundless, then tried repeatedly to burn down their house.

* * *

Because KL offered little in the way of diversion, the English threw lots of parties. The musical 'at home' was a great favourite – the Proudlocks hosted many – as was the formal dinner. This is Sidney's description of a dinner he hosted while heading VI in the early 1920s:

'On the bare shining [dining-room] table is a black porcelain vase [bearing] an electric globe heavily shaded in black and gold.' (The scene seems more appropriate to a seance than it does to a dinner party.) 'I sit at one end of the table with Mrs Hamilton on my right and Miss Boss on my left while Miss Thoroughgood acts as hostess at the other end and is flanked by the two men.' (Miss Boss would have been Josephine Foss, headmistress of the Pudu English Girls' School.) 'Before each of us is a small bowl containing nuts specially fried, and my guests are supposed to eat these before dinner proper begins. Down the table are plates containing apples and oranges and luscious mangosteens while a pineapple flanks the array on one side and a plate of papayas on the other.

'"What piles of fruit," says Mrs Hamilton. "I can't think where you get it all. My cook never seems to be able to get so much."' (Mrs Hamilton, it would appear, is another whose servants are a disappointment to her.)

'Out of the corner of my eye I catch Rah Siaw's expressive face. He is waiting for my signal to bring in the soup.'

Dinner proceeds in desultory fashion and when it is over, 'the boys, silent, white-clad, and gartered above the ankles', serve liqueurs. 'The ladies took cherry brandy or hijou and very soon made a move to the verandah where we heard their subdued conversation.'

The men smoke cigars until the ladies return when Miss Thoroughgood elects to play the piano. 'It was very pleasant to sit back and listen dreamily to one of Chopin's Nocturnes,' Sidney wrote. 'The music seemed to float round the big room and then to escape onto the verandah and so out into the air having become imprisoned first in my brain.'

Now Sidney is asked to sing, which he was all too happy to do, performing 'O Mistress Mine' (in Quilter's setting, we're told), 'Come Away, Death' and 'Songs of a Shropshire Lad', the latter being his party piece.

'The evening had flown away and here it was 11.20, and I thought of 5.15 on the morrow. Not much more than five hours sleep tonight, but it had been worth it.'

Dinner that evening consisted of soup, fish, meat, pudding and cheese. Not, on the face of it, excessive. But consider what had gone before: at 6.30 that morning, Sidney had eaten a biscuit and a banana; at 8.30, fish, bacon and eggs, and toast and marmalade; at 1 p.m., fish, meat, pudding, cheese and coffee; at 4.30, tea with toast and cake; and at 7 o'clock, sardines on toast.

Bilainkin deplored this kind of excess. His tiffin, he said, never consisted of more than a piece of fish and a portion of ice cream. His breakfast, too, he described as modest: two fillets of fish, a large portion of fresh pineapple and six poached or scrambled eggs. That's more than forty eggs a week; some 120 a month; a staggering 1,500 every year.

Friday was mail day, 'a delight always', according to Bilainkin for whom the post meant not just letters from home, but five weekly periodicals (the *Spectator*, *Truth*, the *New Statesman*, *The Economist* and *The Nation*) and parcels of books for review. People looked forward to mail day all week. The mail arrived by train from Penang late on Thursday, was sorted overnight and could be collected on Friday afternoon, but people converged on the post office long before that. By mid-morning, the area around the padang – the post office lay just south of the Secretariat – was packed with cars.

There was much consternation when the mail was late. On

13 January 1910, the *Mail* warned its readers 'that the English mail will probably not be received here until Saturday evening. This delay is no doubt due to the mishap to the P & O s.s. *China* which, while being towed out of Tilbury Docks on December 17, collided with a pier head and sustained extensive damage to her stern and rudder.'

In February 1911, the outgoing mail – letters posted in KL for delivery in England – closed two hours early, catching many people short. The *Mail* was furious. Why hadn't anyone been warned, it wanted to know. In the space of just four weeks, the paper returned to the subject again and again, running in all three editorials in which, using its harshest language, it castigated everyone involved.

For most of these people, the mail was a lifeline, the only connection they had with home. On Fridays, they could thumb through *Punch* and browse the pages of *Country Life* and, for a few short hours, Malaya receded into the background. Doncaster was what concerned them now; and the new play at the Adelphi, and the health of General Booth whose sight was failing . . . Oh, the glory of those Fridays when Malaya was forgotten, and they could imagine themselves back in England, breathing England's air and tramping England's lanes, feeling again the ease that comes when you know a place – its quirks and attitudes and assumptions – and remembering what it means to belong somewhere.

As much as they loved the *Spectator* and the *Illustrated London News*, the British were not great readers. 'Nobody dreams of reading, at any time,' a woman told Bilainkin, 'and if you do, you are thought quaint or funny or touched by the sun.' While Singapore and Penang each had a good library, KL did not. 'For a town of its size and growing tendencies, Kuala Lumpur – in many other ways most up to date – is not at all well-served in this respect,' the *Mail* complained in 1911, 'and the number of books available to the public on serious subjects is practically a negligible quantity.'

KL was prosperous now, made so by the recent rubber boom. Had it wished to, it might have built a decent library. That it didn't has to mean that few really wanted one. Instead, people made do with a book club. Founded in the 1890s and supported by yearly subscriptions, the club steered clear of 'heavy tomes and expensive works of reference', the former because no one cared to read them, and the latter because it lacked for space.

'It was fifty years before we bowed to insistent members' demands to acquire the *Encyclopaedia Britannica*,' Gerald Hawkins would write many years later. 'That was in the early days of WWII and the copy ordered was torpedoed en route.'

The club had 104 members in 1909 (twenty-two fewer than a year earlier) and a collection numbering 1,100 volumes, a third of which had been acquired in the previous twelve months. Considering that there were 700 Britons in KL at the time, all complaining that the hours lay heavily on them, it seems likely that whatever else the British were, they were not bookworms.

The club's policy was a simple one. Instead of buying books that no one was going to read, it purchased only those volumes its members specifically requested. This is what makes the acquisition lists, published each month in the *Mail*, so revealing of British tastes. On the evidence, Ruskin's *Sesame and Lilies* and Stephen's *An Agnostic's Apology* – if it belonged to the club at all – were rare exceptions. From their titles, most of these books appear to have been bodice-rippers. In December 1909, recent additions included *Adventures of a Pretty Woman*, *Breath of Scandal*, *The Love Thief*, *Return of the Petticoat*, *Sidetracks on Bridle Paths*, *The Street of Adventure* and *Strange Stories from a Chinese Studio*.

Over the years, titles like these dominated one list after another. In 1910: *The Love Brokers, The Show Girls, The Wanton*; in 1911: *Diary of My Honeymoon, The Passionate Elopement, The Wages of Sin.* They bring to mind another library, this one belonging to Isherwood's Arthur Norris whose 'very amusing books' included *The Girl with the Golden Whip, Miss Smith's Torture Chamber*, and *Imprisoned at a Girls' School, or The Private Diary of Montague Dawson, Flagellant.*

Could it be said of *The Love Brokers* and *Breath of Scandal* that they assuaged, however briefly, the loneliness of those who read them? Most books, one suspects, fell short for the same reason Arthur Norris's did: 'Their authors adopted a curiously prudish, snobby, lower-middle-class tone, and despite their sincere efforts to be pornographic, became irritatingly vague in the most important passages.' Even so, people do seem to have taken them seriously. Members often complained that books were difficult to read because previous borrowers had filled the margins with annotations – though what marginalia *Diary of My Honeymoon* might inspire is open to conjecture.

Another book acquired in 1910 was *The Wife of Col. Hughes* by Hubert Wales. The story, about a married woman who betrays her husband and has an affair, so closely parallels Mrs Proudlock's own, that it is tempting to speculate that she might not only have read it, but have been inspired by it as well. (That note of hers read to the court in which she said she would rather die than see her name sullied is couched in the kind of language Wales used.) The heroine is Aimée, 'a little pagan with French eyes' and a passion for chocolates, who, like Ethel, is in her early twenties and loves clothes. She is married to Chester Hughes, an MP. But Chester is a dullard, even if his income *is* over five figures. (At dinner he likes to discuss the Balkans.) Aimée is bored stiff – as Mrs Proudlock would have been. And then she meets Howard Keith, a successful artist whose masterpiece is a canvas he calls 'The Sinners'. Aimée equivocates. 'Every day now was . . . a torture of indecision . . . She knew Howard was waiting; she knew that Chester (growing more and more suspicious) was unhappy.' Then, one afternoon, Howard touches her hand, and her fate is sealed. Aimée 'felt all the tense excitement of the angler when a big fish faintly jerks his line. Her blood leaped in a vivid surging sound. In a second of intuition, she knew that she was no longer offering him meretricious coin, but the ringing metal of her womanhood. All she wanted was to give, give, give.'

Here, the stories diverge. Ethel has her fling, is herself betrayed and commits murder. Aimée, who smokes and refuses to have children, is less conventional. She and Howard abscond to Paris where he tells her, 'You and I are pariahs, my dear.' This Aimée doesn't mind at all, but she worries for him. He is sacrificing so much for her: a wife, his children, a career. Is she being fair to him? No, she decides, she isn't, and makes the decision to kill herself. And so, after sending Howard back to England, she heads for Switzerland and the icy death she's planned for herself. 'The search party found her lying in a little valley of snow among the higher slopes near the foot of the Greppen. She had been caught by a storm or by darkness and had died of exhaustion. Aimée had kept her promises. All her bills were met.' I can imagine Ethel's heart swelling as she read all this. Is this how she would have liked her affair with Steward to end? Sending him back to his mother in Cumberland with orders to forget her while she, in hopes of restoring her honour, takes the soldier's way out? Icy death wasn't possible in Malaya, of course. Unless she went to Cold Storage and hid in one of the freezers.

Meetings of the book club's acquisitions committee were

sometimes acrimonious. One female committee member argued long and hard for a book on birth control – with no success. (There was nothing frivolous about this effort. In the early 1900s, a woman in Malaya who wanted to end a pregnancy tried to induce a miscarriage by crawling backwards upstairs.) Another member lobbied vigorously for books about the circus. Most of these disputes ended in compromise. 'One president', Hawkins remembered, 'was a Roman Catholic who had a taste for erudite sermons by the more eminent of his hierarchy. The lawyer on the board was a communist and wanted books on his own religion. The compromise was usually one volume of sermons and one volume of the works of Lenin.'

The British attitude to books was much the same as their attitude towards church: both they could take or leave. In March 1911, a woman attending a service in St Mary's was shocked to find it almost empty. 'There is in Kuala Lumpur a comparatively large English population,' she said, 'and I should have thought that even a small percentage of the members I have met at the various clubs here would have realized their duty to their God.'

Duty to their God, however, was not a great concern. A year earlier, a clergyman in Penang had complained that the British feared more 'the shrinking of their [rubber] shares than the shrinking of all that is best and holy within them'. Those who did go to church went on Sunday morning. The rest of the day could then be devoted to tennis.

This did not sit well with J. Monteath Thompson, St Mary's chaplain, who often accused his congregation of being godless. The British, always sensitive to criticism, did not like this at all, but what really incensed them was a letter he wrote to the *Mail* in February 1910 in which he complained that a going-away party for a departing Briton had occurred during

Lent. A custom of long standing had been broken, Thompson said, and he hoped that it would not set a precedent. Two months later, the British exacted revenge. It was now Thompson's turn to leave – he and his wife were returning to England – and though the Chinese and Indians in his flock threw parties for him, the British pointedly did not. It was shockingly mean-spirited. Thompson – it was he who had married the Proudlocks – was hurt enough to write to the *Mail* again, this time to complain that the British community 'chose not to take any notice of our departure'.

Thompson had worked hard in Selangor and did not deserve to be humiliated. He and his wife were decent people and, unlike many of their compatriots, they had a sense of humour. Bruce Lockhart spent a weekend with them once. He had come to KL to play rugby and had got very drunk. At breakfast next morning, not only was he hung over, he had lost his voice. Mrs Thompson saw her opportunity. Pretending not to know that he had been drinking and affecting concern for his throat, she insisted he down a bottle of cough syrup. The results, Lockhart wrote, were 'hugely embarrassing'.

In March 1911, Thompson, described as a manly man (that phrase again) with a quiet dignity and a noble mouth, had his chance to even the score. He had been appointed to a living in Croydon and in the course of an interview with a local reporter he was asked how the British in KL measured up morally. The temptation must have been great, but generosity won out. Considering the awful temptations in their surroundings, he said, ironically perhaps, their conduct was 'fairly comparable to that at home'.

The British were famous for being hospitable. One woman claimed that 'bungalows are open day and night and, even when the owners are absent, weary travellers are welcome to enter and call for a drink without question'. But their hospitality had in it an element of competition. This hardly mattered when times were good; they could afford to throw lavish parties. But when they weren't, it was merely stupid. 'It is not necessary to supply your guests with a choice of 20 liqueurs,' the *Mail* admonished. 'One need not blush when caught economizing. To spend money like water is a form of side.'

Side. The word, little used today, means pretentiousness or the action of assuming airs. Side was hard to avoid in Malaya. The British were socially competitive because many of them were socially insecure. There was a lot of talk about the school one had gone to; the blue earned at Cambridge; the holiday home in Devon. A connection to an ancient line took a person far in Malaya. But where did that leave the low-born? What were they to do? One man, writing in *The Planter* and going by the name An Old Bird, had an answer. Invent, he advised. Others do it; why shouldn't you? Tell people that your nephew married a cousin of Lord Northcliffe's, or that your father met Kitchener in the lavatory at Lord's. 'Frightfully nice chap. Kitchener. No side there. Salt of the earth.'

Social nuance was everything in Malaya: the way you dressed, the way you spoke, the cigarettes you smoked, the scotch you drank, the homes you visited, those who visited *your* home, the car you drove, your skill at bridge, the number of letters you got on mail day . . . there was really no end to it. Everything was of account because everything was more than it seemed. Even handshakes were analysed. 'Handshakes are classified as follows,' said an article in the *Mail* in 1922: 'the friendly, the economical, the secretive and the indifferent. The man who offers the tips of his fingers is sly, secretive and cunning. You would do well not to trust him.'

The ideals of these people were largely aristocratic. They admired the patrician's insouciance, his indifference to exertion, his sense of himself as favoured by fortune, his belief that, one way or another, he would not come to grief. This is how they wanted people to see them: as accomplished, at ease in the world, having the confidence to take life in their stride. And so, though few could afford it, they sent their children to school in England, and hinted at private incomes and lived beyond their means. They were living a fantasy. And like all fantasies, this one could only survive if everyone played along.

Sending children to England to be educated seems, on the face of it, rather extravagant, but the British felt they had no choice. The tropical heat took a toll on children, they believed. It sapped their energy and made it hard for them to concentrate. There was another reason. Most of these youngsters had been thoroughly spoiled. 'In Malaya,' said Sidney, 'European children are apt to get the idea, partly because the servants will go out of their way to please them, that they really are little lords.' A few years of boarding school was expected to change that.

When a child left for England, his mother often went along, ostensibly to keep an eye on him. I say 'ostensibly', because some of these women, when they departed Malaya, had no intention of ever going back. Playing chaperone became an alternative to divorce; a way to escape an unhappy marriage.

Children in Malaya saw little of their parents. Much of their time was spent with the servants. Not everyone approved. A woman writing in 1921 accused British mothers of neglecting their young and warned them, in effect, that unless they changed their ways, they would burn in hell. The tone of the piece is extraordinary: ranting and wild-eyed. The writer, it is tempting to think, is off her head. But is she? The article appeared in the *Mail*, a paper serious about its responsibilities. Before running this diatribe, it would have satisfied itself that the charges had some basis in fact. The piece is not well written, but for all that it is oddly fascinating, achieving at times an almost biblical power. It is sufficiently interesting to quote at length.

'The majority of children are left very much – too much – to the custody of the native ayah out here,' the writer begins. 'Some of the mothers allow it because they do not know any better, some because they are born tired. With others, it is out of sight, out of mind. . . . The less some mothers see of their offspring the more they like them.'

Mothers, she goes on, would rather spend their time drinking cocktails and smoking Turkish cigarettes 'saturated with saltpetre. Adulteration is inhaled and exhaled defiling dainty lips and, incidentally, God's landscape.

'Some mothers bring their children to the clubs in the principal towns . . . but too often they are left behind. I frequently see a row of mems at this or that out-station club watching the tennis or the cricket. Where are the children? Shopping is done, gymkhanas, and the band playing in the gardens is enjoyed. Again, where are the kiddies?

'The change of a hotel or a shop tiffin, tea or ices is indulged in two or three times a month. Again, where are the children? I have even known fond parents who went away for a week or more, not ill but for a change, to shop in Singapore or Penang. Again, where are the children? The answer is invariably obvious. Left on the mat on the verandah probably with tears in their eyes and sobs choking their hearts that they were left behind . . . refusing the hastily slung-together supper, lying wide-eyed in their cots.'

Like these women's kitchens, 'their nurseries are often unexplored, and the children . . . left to be doped to sleep, smacked to wakefulness, and joggled after food.' (Asian nannies often gave children small doses of opium to keep them quiet.)

'Some mems will do anything to obtain an amah and having obtained it [*sic*] will go to any lengths to keep her. I even know of two ladies who returned from the opera to find their respective new amahs worn out with the day's fatigue – poor dears – sleeping on their mistresses' beds. They were spoken to crossly and retained!

'Many, many poor kiddies have to sleep in a room with their ayahs in this country. Sometimes three children and two ayahs, and I often wonder if the mothers realize this means closed windows and the emanations from perspiring and oleaginous, inadequately washed bodies being inhaled by the innocent and unsuspecting child during the night.'

Referring to what she calls 'the criminal carelessness of the so-called mother', she continues, 'to the mother who is not used to servants, I will say this: if you can't command, if you have no presence, no superiority, no birth, do it yourself and save the wasteful wages.

'There is a serious aspect about all of this. I know of a famous Indian judge who is now a chronic invalid from being constantly doped as a baby, and another man died in fearful agony at the age of 40 through being dropped as a baby by an amah. I once caught . . . an amah doping the baby I was looking after for a friend. Had it been my own child, she would have gone down the back stairs without using her feet. Her own mistress . . . kept her on.

'Tamil ayahs . . . are very fond of smacking babies of all ages. The unmerciful way ignorant Chinese and Tamils of the coolie class smack their own children . . . proves that in some ways the lower animals have more sense. I suppose an amah is not going to have her sleep disturbed if the investment of a few cents per month on a tiny phial [of opiates] is going to bring immunity from nocturnal trouble. *The Bible tells us to honour our fathers and our mothers* [her italics]. Perhaps the negligent ones will be dealt with hereafter. I hope and believe so.'

And there this remarkable screed ends.

Not all mothers were delinquent, of course, nor were all amahs abusive. But to say that doesn't make the picture this woman paints any less chilling. It is significant, too, that her claims weren't challenged. The *Mail*'s readers loved writing letters to the editor. Their holding fire this time suggests that she'd exposed a truth: British children, even if they did live like lords, can't have been terribly happy.

10

'Tragic Wives'

Before Ethel Proudlock took that part-time job and before she fell for William Steward, how did she fill her day? Like most memsahibs, she passed her time in idleness, as inert as that painted ship on Coleridge's painted ocean.

Because few women worked outside the home, they had little to occupy them. Critics said they played bridge all day and traded gossip – charges the mems were quick to deny. Asian servants were notoriously lazy, they claimed, and needed constant supervision. It was as much as they could do to keep them on their toes. This was disingenuous. These homes were not Chatsworth; they were small bungalows of four or five rooms that a person of average ability and vigour could clean more than adequately in a couple of hours. Asian servants did not need to be monitored round the clock. Time lay heavily on them as well, but what they did, they did thoroughly. Not that they had much choice. Mem had an eye like a hawk. Fall short and they could lose their jobs.

The woman who goes to Malaya, Beverley Nicholls wrote in 1931, finds there 'a dignified position [and] an ample and a leisured life . . . She is definitely of the ruling class. [She] has really very little to do except amuse herself.' It sounds quite enviable, but these women didn't think so. In 1928, a Singapore woman said she and thousands like her spent their days 'pale and bored, listlessly wandering through the shops, gathering at noon to hold depressing pahit parties and trying to drink away ennui with gin and bitters'. When night fell, they played 'feverish bridge for heavy stakes'. Or they tried their hand at dancing, their partners 'young bachelors fresh from home who retain their northern vigour and insouciance'.

In England, 'the tragic wives of Malaya' became the stuff of scandal. And with reason. The charges laid against them were largely true. They did go to pot; they did make mischief; they did slander one another. Richard Curle, who visited British communities all over the East, said the gossip in KL was unusually malevolent. But 'what can you expect', he asked, 'when you put women in these unnatural surroundings?'

Curle was wrong about the surroundings. They weren't unnatural at all. What *was* unnatural was the way these women responded to them. They withdrew. No doubt, they had come to Malaya determined to make the best of it, to take an interest in the place, to explore its culture and even, perhaps, learn a language or two. But in the majority of cases, that resolve came to nothing.

Shortly after arriving in Malaya, most women became apathetic – a response dictated not just by the climate, but by the need to fit in. Since everyone else was moaning, since everyone else talked of leaving at the first opportunity, it simply wouldn't do to express enthusiasm for the place. People might think one odd, disloyal or even vulgar.

In Malaya, one could not afford to offend people. One was far from home, a member of a small community, and probably lonely. So one tried to get along, even if it meant associating with people whose company was uncongenial. One smiled when one didn't care to smile and was jolly even when it took an effort. In time, it all came to seem quite natural. To survive in Malaya – morally and spiritually – was a challenge requiring enormous resources: character, patience, independence, generosity of spirit ... It is hardly surprising that so many fell short.

Getting along in KL was especially important. Most of the men were civil servants whose advancement depended on their ability to conform. In the more remote out-stations, eccentric behaviour might be indulged. Not in the federal capital, though. Here, people were watched all the time: at work, at church, at the club, on the sports field. To display any idiosyncrasy at all was to attract the wrong kind of attention. And the wrong kind of attention could stall a career. In Kuala Lumpur, convention was not just important; convention was everything.

As tough as this was on the men, it was even tougher on their wives who had to endure not just the constraints peculiar to their role as the bearers of progress, but a second set of restrictions, these having to do with Edwardian notions of female propriety. Women were shown the greatest respect and treated with elaborate courtesy, but it was required of them that they be little more than decorative. What's more, few of them had any education. Ruskin was of the opinion that women didn't need schooling; that they evolved the same way flowers did: without effort. Send a woman to school, he said, and all you got for your pains was a walking dictionary.

'In the Far East, the white woman counts for very little,' Nicholls wrote. 'The East is a man's world.' Certainly, it seemed that way. Men held all the power. Men received all the glory. Theirs was the satisfaction of knowing that they had transformed 'a strange and hostile country into a happy and prosperous dependency'. Women were involved in this Grand

Endeavour only tangentially: they provided their men with moral support.

It doesn't sound nearly as interesting as drafting budgets and making policy, but some wives defended even this limited role. Responding to Nicholls, a woman wrote in the *Mail* that, to an extent unimaginable at Home, wives in Malaya could, depending on their disposition, make or break their husbands. 'The personality of a wife here has far more influence on her husband's career than it has in England,' she said. 'The woman who makes a public nuisance of herself in Malaya is damning her husband's future.' (Ethel Proudlock is a prime example.) 'Even the innocently stupid woman who makes enemies from ignorance can do harm.'

There was more involved, however, than simply abetting a man's career. By being supportive, a woman affected her husband's outlook, buoyed his spirits and kept at bay that most dreaded of tropical ailments, neurasthenia. Referring to Malaya's staggering suicide rate, this woman added: 'If we look back on the cases of tragedy which occur from time to time, we shall find almost certainly that they do not happen to a man whose wife is with him.'

Whose wife is with him . . . How Ruskinesque that sounds. Perhaps she is another who had read 'In Queens' Gardens', with its notion of the home as 'the place of peace; the shelter . . . from all terror, doubt and division.'

When not providing emotional and moral support, a woman in Malaya had precious little else to do. The job of raising children and keeping house – tasks that, in England, would have filled her time – were not available to her. Servants did all that. Why, in that case, did she not rid herself of servants and do her *own* chores? That option was not available, either. If she did that, a woman lost caste. As intolerable as her situation was *with* servants, without them it would only have been worse.

Oh, if they'd only stayed in England, the women said, how much happier they would have been. And maybe they were right. Women were circumscribed in England, too, but their lives would have been more varied. They would not have had to see the same faces every day; would not have had to have the same conversations. And they would have been less conspicuous. In Malaya, they were constantly on display, constantly on their guard. That was the worst of it: pretending to be a paragon. Because they were there to set an example, they could never be short of exemplary.

Why, then, did not more of them go home? There were several reasons: inertia, loyalty, fear . . . Going home would have meant leaving their husbands and having to support themselves; it would have meant an end to all that comfort; it would have meant a loss of status. No servants now, no men dancing attendance. In Malaya, white women 'are queens, though the crowns disappear as soon as they approach the shores of England,' Bilainkin wrote. 'I saw striking confirmation [of this] at Wimbledon. A woman who was always sure in Malaya of a large circle of men friends . . . stood alone with her husband. Her ordinary afternoon frock caught nobody's attention . . . It must have seemed incredible to her proud eyes that not a man turned towards her. London was teaching the returned wanderer a stern lesson.'

As much as they hated Malaya – as much as they longed for their old lives – there could be no retreat. In their hearts, they knew this, and it made their situation even more agonizing. Some women chose to sit and brood. Others did their brooding in bed, retiring to their rooms when their husbands left for work in the mornings and staying there till lunch was ready. It was a deadly life, and women were not to be blamed for detesting it. In the circumstances, it seems curious that it was almost always the men who went off their heads and killed themselves. Women endured – but what an awful endurance it must have been. Growing daily more bored, daily more disenchanted, they created misery not just for themselves but for everyone around them.

Very few of them had female confidantes. They saw each other all the time – they patronized the same clubs, played the same sports, went to the same parties – but intimacy eluded them. Intimacy requires candour, and that was barred to them. Candour would have given the game away, would have threatened the fiction that it was *noblesse oblige* alone that kept them here, a spirit of Victorian self-sacrifice. England expected every man – and every woman, too – to do their duty. And this they did, or pretended to, with knuckles white and teeth gritted.

Malaya, it was stressed again and again, was a man's world. It was only recently that women had begun to arrive in any numbers. Until 1905, conditions had been considered too harsh, too primitive. Even in 1920, when conditions had begun to improve, Malaya was still considered no fit place for a female. Women did not flourish there; if anything, they seemed to deteriorate. In *The Planter* in 1923, 'Arnold' claimed that 'temperamentally, most women change for the worse out here', an alteration he blamed on a life of ease and indolence. 'One rapidly becomes, to say the least of it, somewhat difficult. Frequently this mental change is accompanied by a physical one. There are those who become stout and those who become thin.' The stout ones, he went on, are sticklers for etiquette who give formal dinner parties and require their guests to wear 'erstwhile Piccadilly glad rags. Not even a heat wave will force [them] to dispense with an iota of pomposity.' The thin ones were even worse, compensating for their loss of weight 'by increased energy – all too frequently misdirected'.

According to 'Arnold', women in Malaya for any length of time abandoned the 'feminine niceties': 'They do let themselves get dull – as dull as Hades – and retain as much sparkle of real life as a jelly fish would beer.' Even sadder, many of them were unaware of it. Arnold recalled often seeing 'some chalk-faced, emaciated, flat-chested, self-styled old stager endeavour to assuage the fears of a new arrival with, "Ah, don't you worry, my dear. I've been out here three years now, and look at me".'

'Well,' he finished, 'it has its funny side, but there is a heap of tragedy in it also.'

Men often accused women of dressing badly, and some criticized their persons. 'Think of all those bare arms and shoulders at the club dance, few of them up to artist's models' specifications,' one man wrote. 'Think of those many shaped calves and ankles displayed mostly, let us hope, in entire ignorance of their lack of artistic appeal to the exacting eye.'

Men, it should be remembered, were no feast for the eye, either. (One woman complained that, as well as not shaving regularly, their suits were rumpled, their collars were ragged and their shoes were ever in need of polish.) But women were held to a different standard. Not only had they to look attractive, they were expected to charm, to beguile, to amuse. Their job, they were given to understand, was to be an asset to a man, to be a consolation to him, to bless him with offspring. It was a tall order.

A significant number of men in Malaya neither trusted women nor liked them very much. Misogyny was rife. Men spent much of their time with other men. Their wives saw them hardly at all. Couples ate together, and went to the club together but, once there, they parted company, the women to talk on the verandah, and the men to drink in the bar – an all-male preserve. (On the morning of the murder, Will Proudlock met at different times with no fewer than three of his male friends and, that night, had dinner with a fourth.)

Until about 1910, life in Malaya, with its peculiar living arrangements (bachelors lived four or five to a house), its contact sports and its male camaraderie, resembled in many ways life in a public school. Whether there was an element of homo-eroticism in any of this is open to question, but what does seem certain is that many men resented the appearance of women in their midst. They would have known of the campaign, then underway in England, to encourage middle-class women to emigrate, the belief being that their presence overseas would raise moral standards. That was the last thing men wanted. Women were seen as spoilers, bad sports who threatened a way of life.

Adding to male unease was the campaign for women's suffrage being waged in England. When, in August 1910, E. A. O. Travers suggested a meeting in the Spotted Dog to discuss the subject of votes for women, he cannot have anticipated the uproar it would unleash. Letters to the *Malay Mail*, usually phrased so carefully, set new standards for vitriol. The suffragettes (referred to as the 'shrieking sisterhood') were denounced as criminals and gaolbirds as writer after writer expressed his horror at 'the spectacle of mobs of unsexed creatures' battling policemen in the streets of London.

There was little support in KL for women's rights. When not considered actually dangerous, suffragettes were seen as figures of fun. In *The Arcagettes*, H. R. Shaw played Susan Shocker, a feminist so preposterous, he stopped the show. 'Mr. Shaw's song "Susan" met with a great reception,' the *Mail* said on 17 April, 'and the dance that followed was encored so often that it nearly proved fatal to the poor man.' The presence of Sir John Anderson on 30 April seems to have spurred Shaw to even greater efforts. His performance that night, the *Mail* reported, 'sent the house into screams'.

The anti-feminists must have thought themselves on firm

ground. No less a person than Queen Victoria had vilified the suffrage movement. Dismissing women's rights as a 'mad, wicked folly', she accused the suffragettes of forgetting 'every sense of womanly feeling and propriety . . . Woman would become the most hateful, heartless – and disgusting – of human beings were she allowed to unsex herself!'

(How the reactionaries must have quaked when, in February 1927, M. Paul Poiret, 'that great monarch of the world of women's fashions', announced in the *Mail* that skirts were doomed. 'In thirty years' time, women will wear trousers,' said the Paris dress designer, 'and skirts will be as much things of the past as is long hair today.')

It was not only the men who regarded women with hostility; the women did not much like one another, either. At the club, Arnold said, 'all the mems are bundled together looking thoroughly bored while endeavouring to hide their real feelings for each other under a constant flow of small talk'.

Men were largely to blame for the predicament in which women found themselves. Many, when they went to England in search of a wife, exaggerated Malaya's qualities. These men had had their fill of loneliness. They wanted homes and they wanted children so desperately that they didn't mind lying. (Because nurses were considered an easy mark, men seeking wives often spent their leave lurking around teaching hospitals.)

Such men came in for special condemnation from Mrs John Bruce, the wife of a prominent planter. 'He boasts to his fiancée of his fine billet, his beautiful bungalow,' she complained in *The Planter* in 1920. 'Nothing for her to do but enjoy herself.' And what happened? 'The fiancée comes out, finds everything but the expected paradise and, giving the country a short month's trial, packs up and goes home. And the world says of such [men], "Serves him right." Instead of merely giving the good points of Malaya, such a man should take care to emphasize its loneliness, its insects, its many drawbacks.'

While men often misled women as to what was in store for them, it was probably the case as well that some women were all too eager to be taken in. Because of a rubber boom in 1910, word had begun to spread in England that Malaya was an El Dorado, a place so rich in resources that even the inept were making fortunes. Malaya, the subject of so many myths, had spawned one more – much to the amusement of *The Planter.* Tongue firmly in cheek, it advised intending immigrants that 'before coming out, essentials should be concentrated upon such as an easily portable pianola, a cocktail shaker, bed warmer for airing the mattress, Wellington boots, polo sticks, three saucepans (if married, four) and two or three dainty . . . dressing-table covers. Lastly, money and gloves.'

When they realized that Malaya was not as they had pictured it, women did not always pack their bags and go home. Some had affairs and *then* went home. In January 1923, Edwin William Waterfield was granted a decree nisi dissolving his marriage to Madge Waterfield on the grounds that she and William Forsyth had committed adultery. Waterfield told a London court of warning Forsyth to stay away from his wife, and Forsyth had promised that he would, assuring Waterfield (known as Billy) that he meant to 'play the game'. But the attraction proved too great and, in 1920, less than a year after the Waterfields had married, Madge and Forsyth fled to England.

From London, Madge sent her husband an anguished letter. 'I would give half my life to undo the wrong I did you when I married you,' she wrote. 'I have tried ever so hard to forget him altogether . . . I cannot give him up, and yet I am tied to you. My dear Billy, it was just fate that I should fall in love with him, and he with me. I am damn sorry for you, Billy, and I am damn sorry for myself, too. I can never come back to you, Billy, so I am asking you to set me free. God bless you.'

Mrs Bruce would not have liked Madge. She believed that whoever you were – and whatever your circumstances – it was incumbent upon you to make the best of things. *The Planter* thought the world of her. 'Her brave philosophy,' it enthused, 'teaches the value of hard work as an antidote to the boredom that comes at times to all mems in Malaya.'

Mrs Bruce had a special dislike of idlers. It was true, she said, there *were* women who didn't pull their weight; women who took to their beds when their husbands left for work. 'There are slackers amongst us,' she thundered. 'But buck up, sisters. See to it that we do not fritter away our time in frivolous reading or idly criticizing our neighbours.'

How, then, might a woman employ herself? Lots of ways, barked Mrs Bruce: 'Life is full of interest, whether we live on isolated estates or are surrounded by neighbours. [I]t is up to us women to make the most of our lives, to encourage and cheer our men, to leave the world a little better than we find it.'

Mrs Bruce then got down to practicalities. The hours between breakfast and tiffin could be long, she admitted, 'but for those who are fond of dusting and superintending the ordinary cleaning of the house and also of sewing, the forenoon is never too long. I have heard one or two women say that the mornings are endless and that they hate sewing, but surely each of us can find a hobby of some sort – sketching or painting, writing or typing – anything but being idle.'

'Those who are fond of dusting . . .' Dear Mrs Bruce. Admirable though she was, her thinking does seem a bit reductive. She seems honestly to have believed that it took very little to make a woman happy: just a dirty house and a feather duster.

Five months later, she was on the attack again. Describing women as 'somewhat expensive luxuries', her complaint this time was their lack of thrift: '[I]t is up to us women to cut down expenses in every direction, to stifle our wish to buy unnecessary dainties and confine ourselves to absolute necessities. It is to us our menfolk look to cheer them up, to keep their minds off their worries and to keep our own small worries and petty jealousies to ourselves.' Men, no doubt, exulted when they read this, though it can hardly have endeared her to her 'sisters'.

Many marriages soured, it was believed, because men were apt to wed in haste. The typical man had six months' leave every four or five years, and two of those months were spent at sea, which did not give him a lot of time. Men in England might spend years choosing a wife; if they were lucky, men in Malaya had sixteen weeks (hence the importance of teaching hospitals).

Time being short, many men, with little opportunity to explore a woman's character, opted instead for looks. Wrong, wrong, wrong, said Winstedt. What a wife needed was not a face that made hearts flutter on a P. & O., but 'a face that can endure ten thousand rubber trees for its background'. Life on a rubber estate made special demands on a woman, which is why planters seeking marriage were urged to exercise care. City girls would not do at all, they were told. A woman accustomed to the amenities of a place like London could never adjust to life in the jungle. 'What in heaven's name is that unfortunate girl to do?' asked *The Planter.* 'Just this: to sit and brood and cultivate a bitter hatred for the country and the people and, in many cases, for the man' who brought her to this sorry pass.

A much safer bet was a country lass: a girl who took difficulties in her stride and who would not mind if the oil lamps smoked and the plumbing did not work. Such a person 'will probably find life on a rubber estate great fun', *The Planter* said, 'and she will certainly surround herself with animals and try to have her own poultry yard and her garden and possibly a cow or two.'

The rural idyll this suggests – one is reminded of Marie Antoinette and her ladies playing at being shepherdesses – is clearly misleading. But *The Planter* was making a serious point. 'For a man to marry the wrong type of woman and to bring her to the tropics is rather like caging a lioness in the zoo,' it warned. 'She will live and sleep and eat and may even reproduce her species, but given the chance she will turn round and rend her keeper and destroy him if she can.'

How chilling that sounds. The woman who claimed that a caring wife was all that stood between a man and suicide was telling only half the story; there must have been times as well when an uncaring woman made a man wish he were dead. Malaya's disgruntled wives much exercised the *Mail*. 'The tropics are not a white woman's country,' it admitted in November 1922, but for all that, it said, women in Malaya had a far better time of it than their counterparts in Africa or Australia or even Canada: 'Most women in this part of the world never forget that they are exiles and constantly talk about the fuller, better and more interesting life they can live at Home.'

In England, these women would probably have lived in a London suburb. Did they really think they would be happier in Fulham? They complained that KL had no music to speak of and no theatre, quite forgetting they had no appetite for either. They liked to imagine themselves thronging the Royal Opera House and jostling for seats in the Albert Hall, but this was make-believe. They were philistines, a fact that going back to England was unlikely to change.

They said there was nothing to do in Malaya. But this was

nonsense, too, said the *Mail.* There was no end of possibilities, 'allowing for absolutely selfish people who think only of themselves and the irreconcilables who can see no good in anything in a country they have made up their minds to dislike'.

Why this extraordinary animus? The pain of exile was one reason; and the so-called awful conditions (which really were not all that bad); and the absence of any intimacy. They also disliked Malaya because everyone else disliked it, and because now Malaya was all they had. As much as they pined for Home, Home, they realized, no longer pined for them. 'We go to England as fashion orders, for a holiday and are soon tired,' one man said. 'After a few years, nobody remembers us, or wants us. Nobody cares about us at home.' And, finally, they disliked Malaya because, as all new places do, it presented them with a challenge that few were able to meet. Malaya was bigger than they were. And that rankled.

Not all women who left England to live abroad behaved like this. Those who went to Canada and New Zealand were a different breed. Typical was Catherine Dahm, a contemporary of Mrs Proudlock's. The wife of a sheep farmer, Dahm had nine children, delivering most of them herself. From her, they learned to read and write and learned as well the importance of work. Her life was full because she was always occupied, baking bread, making clothes, tending a vegetable garden, running a store, operating a post office. She was liked by everyone and got on famously with her Maori neighbours.

What distinguished Dahm and others like her was their toughness. They were robust, energetic, enterprising and, in many cases, working class. So, too, were the early women settlers in Africa. They did not repair to clubs in the evenings, and they did not rely on servants. If something needed doing, they pitched in and did it themselves. The women in these places – and this, finally, is what set them apart – were participants. They were engaged, deeply involved in the life around them.

Why didn't people like Dahm go to Malaya? Because they were not wanted there. Malaya was small and could be run by a small cadre of middle-class professionals. It did not need England's poor. The FMS had plenty of servants, and what labourers were needed, first by the tin mines and later by the rubber estates, could be found closer to hand in China and in southern India.

The British government encouraged the working classes to emigrate to places like Canada and the antipodes, sometimes even providing them with free or assisted passages. Not to Malaya, though. To get to Malaya, people paid their own way. And that was just the half of it. To succeed there, they also needed social credentials. Lack those, and they were likely to wish that they had stayed at home.

11

Rubber Fever

The planter's life was tough. He worked long, and he worked hard, often in terrible conditions. Those living in remote areas were especially vulnerable. Many fell ill, became alcoholics or, tiring of the loneliness, took their own lives. While, in 1911, places like KL and Ipoh could boast such amenities as the telephone and the cinema, the planter was making do with *stengahs* and solitude.

The planter rose early – usually at 5 a.m. – and had done a day's work by the time he sat down to breakfast four hours later. First, his labourers were inspected, and then he made his rounds: checking equipment, examining trees, instructing work crews. After breakfast, he repaired to the factory, and after lunch, it was the office that claimed his time. Nor was he done when he got home in the evenings. Once dinner was out of the way, there were records to update – an onerous task made doubly so by the virtual absence of light. 'Adding up columns of figures in the dark was an unpleasant and tedious duty,' one man wrote. By the time the planter had finished, he was often too tired to sleep and 'gulped sufficient imported whisky or brandy to drown his fatigue'.

Estates were run as if they were army posts. From the time the gong summoned workers to muster in the mornings until dwindling light forced the last weeding party back to the labour lines, it was expected that everyone would give of their best. Discipline was everything, and those who fell short were shown no mercy. Planters, dressed in their customary shorts and knee-length socks, were famous for their lack of patience. If even one worker made a mistake, the brunt was borne by all. The planter's 'foul temper . . . raged through the entire plantation', one man wrote. 'Everyone could feel and share the tremors.'

The planter and his family, if he had one, lived in a small bungalow which, in the early days, boasted neither electricity nor running water. Light was provided by oil lamps which smoked appallingly, and one washed in rain water collected in barrels. Smoking lamps were the least of it, though; altogether worse were the insects. 'There is something dreadful about opening a packet of flour and finding it crawling with cockroaches,' wrote one planter's wife. 'Every time you put sugar into your tea, you see drowning white ants struggling on top. You never get used to them really, although you may fish them out with an expert spoon.'

There were red ants as well, invading your person 'as if one was a lump of carrion', and sandflies which bit without buzzing. 'You can no more ignore their sting than you could help jumping if pricked unexpectedly with the end of a red hot needle.'

The planter's great enemy was what one man called 'the awful soul-deadening, brain-destroying monotony'. There was respite for a few short hours on Sundays, when many got together for a curry tiffin. 'I generally overate myself', Leopold Ainsworth wrote, 'before sleeping like a pig throughout the long afternoon.' And there was payroll day which meant a trip into town to visit the bank. Many planters chose to make an occasion of it. Lockhart would head for the Sungei Ujong Club in Seremban where he 'imbibed vast quantities of gin pahits'. In the Spotted Dog, *pahits* were dispatched as well, and the scene was often boisterous. Henri Fauconnier described one such gathering in *The Soul of Malaya*: 'Old Homewood had hoisted himself onto a table and there stood with congested eyes and violent violet cheeks tramping on broken glasses and brandishing a cane chair.'

Sunday afternoons and payroll day aside, planters worked all the time. They had no choice. Since nature did not rest, neither could they. If they once relaxed their efforts, they would be swallowed up. They had succeeded in driving back the wild, but the victory was pyrrhic. Nature's encroachments never ceased; every day, it was necessary to drive it back all over again. The jungle was mocking them. They had not conquered it; it had conquered them. It had reduced them to slaves.

Though the work was often brutal and required little imagination, planters were expected to be both well-educated and well-born. In 1907, an advertisement in *The Times* seeking junior assistants was very specific about this. 'Good birth and education', it said, '*sine qua non*.' One who answered that advertisement was C. R. Harrison who was a mere eighteen years old when he reached Malaya, looking, in his words, 'very pink and white'. A man seeing him smoke a cigar wanted to know, 'Who is that cigar with a boy behind it?'

For all his youth, however, Harrison was resourceful. When cholera struck his estate in 1908, he set to work at once. Every man, woman and child was stripped and washed and disinfected, and everything they owned was burned. It was drastic, but it worked. Only one person died. Ten years later, he proved himself again. This time the problem – as if Malaya did not have enough scourges – was a flu epidemic. 'Those [workers] who were fit enough had to be employed looking after the sick and burying the dead,' Harrison wrote. 'In my own case, I . . . pooled all the milk, brandy and blankets I could find and gave every patient brandy and milk every three hours. I had few deaths.'

A good man, Harrison took seriously the welfare of those who worked for him. So it was with sadness that I discovered this item in the *Mail* in January 1911: 'We learn that Mr Harrison, a Kuala Selangor planter, has been brought into the European Hospital here with his throat cut from the ear to the chin. He was attacked by an assailant while sleeping.' Happily, Harrison survived.

Those planters like Harrison who came to Malaya at the turn of the century were pioneers. It was they who cleared the jungle, and they who nursed the early trees. Tough and enterprising, they were planting's elite and rather looked down on those who succeeded them. The newcomers, they felt, were not the men they had been; they did not have their mettle, nor did they have their *esprit de corps.* After the First World War, one man said, being a planter no longer required that one be 'officer material or ex-public school'. While many growers still *were* public school, others were 'no-school' at all. The war itself had bred resentments. While some planters had served their country, others avoided conscription by claiming disabilities. There were two kinds of planter now: those who had fought and those who had not. The latter were never allowed to live it down. Each time he saw these people on the playing field, a man wrote in 1923, he was always reminded that, when the war broke out, they were 'too malaria-sodden or too weak-hearted' to do their duty.

Planters were expected to be many things: horticulturalists, business managers, book-keepers and linguists. Tamil, though, gave them no end of trouble. (Winstedt called it the language used in hell.) Attempts to speak Malay were not too successful, either. Hearing them, one man said, he was reminded of nuts being cracked. Planters were called on to be father figures, too. Labourers sought their help with all sorts of things. A worker was getting married; did the manager think it a good idea? Or a baby had been born; could the manager suggest a name? Not all managers enjoyed dispensing advice. 'Nothing is more trying than the . . . trivial worries which [the workers] insist on confiding in the planter,' wrote Arthur Keyser. 'The coolie lines are little more than nurseries for grown-up orientals.'

Considering all they had to do, it seems surprising that planters would complain of being bored. Isolation was part of the problem. In the early days, weeks might pass before a planter saw another European. It was the case as well that few planters had any interests. *The Planter* thought this something of a scandal and was for ever urging growers to embrace a hobby. One recommendation was that they learn to cook – this drew howls of derision. Another was stamp-collecting. Philately, the magazine said, 'provides one of the most interesting, restful and, at the same time, remunerative of hobbies'. This did not go down too well either. In 1920, the Malayan Stamp Exchange could boast no more than a hundred members.

Worse than the tedium, though, *The Planter* said in 1923, much, much worse, were the 'nagging epistles from agents and directors airing their ignorance from the comfort of arm chairs'. While Malaya had some proprietary planters, most estates were publicly-owned companies registered in London and controlled by boards of directors. Directors did not operate estates themselves, they left that to agency houses of which

KL had several. The agency house performed a number of functions: it hired and fired managers; it purchased needed materials; and – in the person of the visiting agent – it inspected the estate several times a year to satisfy itself that the manager understood his role in this great enterprise: maximizing profits.

Though some, no doubt, were decent men, visiting agents generally, as well as the directors they represented, were roundly hated. Most, having been growers themselves, were free with their advice, and this the planters resented. They alone knew their estates, they believed; and it galled them that an outsider would try to tell them how to run them. To some extent, they had a point. In many ways, each estate was unique, which meant that a practice that had worked on one might fail on another or even prove disastrous on a third. This put a planter in some difficulty. If he ignored the agent, he stood to lose his job, but doing as he was told also involved some risk. What if the agent were wrong? What if yields fell? If that happened, the planter was likely to lose his job as well.

Of the two, most planters decided that buckling under was the safer course. They did so grudgingly. Agents, they complained, were arbitrary and undermined their authority; they were sadists whose chief satisfaction was driving them to drink. The war between the two groups became so acrimonious that, in 1922, the *Straits Times* – known as the Colonial Thunderer – urged company directors to strip agents of some of their powers. 'We would suggest to the agents that a little more respect for men on the spot and a little more recognition of their own limitations would be welcome,' the paper said. 'Too many agents make the lives of the managers who serve under them a misery.'

Directors posed a problem, too. So controlling were they, so intrusive, that planters had to seek their permission when they wanted to marry. Growing rubber was a full-time job, the companies contended. If a planter married, it was inevitable that his work would suffer. At least one planter defied this rule and paid dearly for it. Fired from his job and unable to find another, N. C. Begg despaired and, in December 1927, tried to commit suicide. He told a court in Singapore that he had wanted to die for some time and, for the purpose, had purchased a bottle of barbiturates, but it was only when a promised job fell through that he was moved to act.

That job had been withdrawn after he and his wife were ordered to leave the Europe Hotel. They had gone there to eat and had been seated near the ladies' cloakroom. This, the court was told, infuriated Mrs Begg who, using 'extremely filthy language' and in a loud voice, began to expound, most unflatteringly, on the morality of British women. They left when asked to but an hour later they returned, and Mrs Begg resumed her discourse, filled this time with 'disgusting expressions'. That was when the police were called. A day later, Begg went to Johore for a job interview, but word of the incident had preceded him, and the job was given to someone else. It was then he decided to kill himself. He went to a bar, drank several whiskies and ingested twenty-five barbiturates.

Begg, whose only income was £100 sent to him every month by his mother in England, was bound over after promising the court that he would not try to kill himself again. It is unclear what became of him. A representative of the St Andrew's Society offered to buy him a ticket home but, as the offer did not include his wife, it was declined. Mrs Begg had stuck by him for seven years, he said. He had no intention of deserting her now.

The indignities suffered at the hands of agents and directors might have seemed less onerous had planters been paid more. It was growers who had 'turned thousands of acres of damp and reeking jungle' into some of the best agricultural land in the world, *The Planter* claimed in 1923. 'And yet the planter has collectively derived less pecuniary benefit from his labours than the nest of parasites who have battened fat on the industry.' The 'parasites' – the directors said to be engorging themselves in London – bore some of the blame. The planters, though, cast a wider net. In their view, the government was at fault as well. It had failed to represent their interests.

This was not entirely fair. As even *The Planter* had to admit, it was 'largely through the energy and the enterprise of our legislative assemblies that in recent years rubber and tin and the prosperity of everyone of every race in Malaya has developed faster than similar races and similar industries in any other portion of the globe'. But in 1925, when the charge of official neglect was being made, passions were running high. Rubber smuggling had been a problem for years, but recently it had intensified. Organized gangs had charge of the traffic now, and some estates were losing as much as a quarter of their output every month. The planters demanded action, but the government insisted there was nothing it could do. The growers seemed to be asking, it said, that it put a policeman under every rubber tree which, if they thought about it, they could not fail to realize was beyond its resources. The planters were understandably furious. One more perfidy, they said. Why was it that, again and again, they got short shrift?

It was not only government policies that drew the ire of planters; it was government officials as well. On average, civil servants earned more than growers did, and they enjoyed more prestige. This, though, is not how the planters would have put it. According to them, civil servants had grown too high and mighty. They hinted as well that they did not do an awful lot. They were time-servers, planters said; people whose only interest was their next raise and their next promotion.

In January 1923, a man writing in *The Planter* described a government servant as someone 'whose office duties interfere seriously with golf and bridge, at homes, card-shooting and other healthful past times'. Just a few months later, he was on the attack again. 'The government men out here', he said, 'are the salt of the earth and, like salt, they are excellent fellows in small quantities and serve a good purpose, but too much of it is distasteful.'

Even their wives came in for disdain. If, when shopping, you see a lady 'looking severely plain in skirt and blouse and masculine topee', another contributor wrote, 'it is three-to-one that she is a government mem – the wife, that is, of a more or less hardworking cadet who thinks she has a mission in life which is to set an example in economy as from the high-born to those other vain creatures whose husbands are merely merchants or lawyers or planters'.

Civil servants needed to be reminded, one man said, that they were in Malaya for the same reason planters were: to get rich. 'Let us be honest and admit that we're all after the spondulicks,' he went on. 'Some of us may not be as brazen or as unscrupulous as some others . . . But let anyone put us on to easy money, and we are all at it like flies around a jam pot.'

The planters were fooling no one. What really irked them about civil servants was their suspicion that officials looked down on them. While members of both groups had gone to public schools, officials were more likely to have attended the better ones. And unlike planters, most officials had been to university – in many cases Oxford or Cambridge. Some, like Richard Winstedt and R. J. Wilkinson and, more recently, Victor Purcell and J. M. Gullick, immersed themselves in Malaya and became important scholars. Planters had no time for scholarship. Aggressively anti-intellectual, they prided themselves on being gruff and hearty and down to earth. Mention poetry around them, and they were apt to call you Powder Puff Percy. Bruce Lockhart avoided them as much as he could. He called them dullards and said he preferred the company of officials. 'I showed them my poems. They invited me to admire their watercolours.'

Planters, Lockhart complained, rarely read a book, and when they did it was never very challenging. 'The average planter's library might contain a varied selection of the prose and poetry of Kipling, but its chief stand-by . . . was the works of Hubert Wales and James Blyth.' Lockhart, a planter himself, was the exception proving the rule. He set great store by reading. Were it not for his library, he said, he could never have avoided the Eastern Trinity: opium, drink and women.

Among Lockhart's books was one called *Twentieth Century Impressions of British Malaya.* Published in 1908, it is not a distinguished work, and I mention it only because of a prediction it made: 'The hinterland of the [Malay] peninsula bids fair to become a veritable commercial El Dorado.' A mere two years later it did just that. 'The rubber industry is booming,' the *Mail* announced on 21 February 1910, all thanks to the new car industry and its need of rubber tyres. 'New rubber companies are being floated all the time.' And they were – sometimes as many as five a day, but even this was insufficient to meet demand. Stock brokers said they had seen nothing like it. The clamour for shares was unprecedented. 'The rubber boom is more feverish than ever,' the *Mail* reported happily on 24 February. 'The carry-over is in indescribable confusion.'

On 1 March, there were nine new flotations – a record for a single day. Rubber had become an obsession, and no one was spared. One man complained that he never saw his newspaper any more. His servants commandeered it – to see how *their* shares were doing. Rubber, rubber, rubber . . . It was all one heard, and some were growing weary of it. 'It would be refreshing to find someone who is willing to talk of something else other than rubber shares,' the *Mail* complained.

London, too, had succumbed to rubber fever. The *Illustrated London News* was full of rubber stories, as was *Punch.* (In one *Punch* cartoon called 'If the Rubber Boom Continues', a man on a golf course reports the loss of his ball to a very grave policeman while, behind him, detectives search the gorse with magnifying glasses, and a bloodhound noses round a sand trap.) The capital had come down with a bad case of rubber madness, the *Sketch* warned on 10 March. In restaurants and in drawing rooms, in offices and on the tube, the topic was always the same: the fortune to be made in rubber shares.

By mid-March, share prices had reached such unprecedented levels that the London Stock Exchange was being called the *shock* exchange. A new malady now made an appearance. Known as rubber throat, its victims were invariably traders and its chief symptom 'a hoarseness caused by the incessant shouting of the latest quotations'.

In early May, a dinner party hosted by a successful London investor boasted an unusual menu: each course was a play on the name of a well-known rubber estate: Consommé Chersonese; Anglo-Malayonnaise with Jugra hare; Kuala Lumpur agneau; pommes de Petaling; and Pears Tremelbye with Vallambrosa ice. The wine list included Merlinum and Singaport.

On 27 April, the boom claimed its first casualty when a thirty-seven-year-old London stock broker named Arthur Septimus Kidd threw himself into the path of a train. He died instantly. At the inquest, Kidd's uncle said it was pressure of work that had driven his nephew to kill himself. Kidd had complained of debilitating headaches, the court was told, a consequence of his working long past midnight. The coroner returned a verdict of suicide while of unsound mind.

In May, the *Mail* announced that rubber prices had experienced a sudden drop. 'Buyers', it said, 'are staying their hand.' And then, on 11 June, one of Selangor's leading estates said it was abandoning rubber and going into coconuts. The average price of No. 1 rubber on 31 December 1909 was seven shillings and fourpence halfpenny. In April, it peaked at twelve shillings and tuppence, nearly twice that. But by the end of the year, it had fallen dramatically, standing at five shillings and sixpence on 31 December. The boom was over.

'Scores' of people in KL and Singapore made huge profits, the *Mail* said. But for many, they were illusory. Because the boom had ended so abruptly, many investors were caught off guard. Bruce Lockhart's grandmother, known in Edinburgh as the Queen of Rubber, was one of many whose fortunes were wiped out almost overnight. But for the several months it lasted, the boom had been a heady experience. Tens of thousands of people had invested in rubber, among them 'royal princesses, clergymen, tradesmen of all kinds, sailors and soldiers, and even inmates in workhouses'. And some lasting good had come of it. The rubber boom, the *Mail* announced, had 'brought the eyes of the whole world upon this hitherto somewhat obscure corner of the empire'. *The Planter* went even further, declaring that 'the boom of 1910 did more than anything to make the Malaya we know today'.

The industry revived during the First World War only to collapse again in 1920. That downturn was particularly severe and caused great hardship. Many planters were thrown not just out of work, but out of their homes as well. A woman writing in *The Planter* was only half-joking when she said that she and her husband might have to work their passage home, he as a stoker and she a stewardess 'turning an honest penny sweeping coursings or something equally genteel'.

Others became even more fatalistic. Early in 1922, a chain letter surfaced in Kuala Lumpur, a city that once had been so pragmatic. It was headed 'Good Luck' and read: 'Copy this out and send it to nine people to whom you wish good luck.' Malaya was clearly growing desperate.

No one was spared, not even those men who had worked day and night for years. As the crisis worsened, whole families were turned into the street. One man, frantic to make a living, opened a shoe-shine stand. The authorities were appalled. White men didn't polish shoes, they said; think of the impact on British prestige. The stand was quickly removed.

The directors in London watched this suffering with indifference. Planters accused them of being callous. That was not fair, the companies said, it was not their job to feed and house people. Their duty lay with their stockholders. In the early 1920s, many rubber companies had large reserves of cash, but instead of disbursing emergency aid, they used them instead to pay their investors a dividend.

For many growers, it was a sobering experience. The Incorporated Society of Planters, often accused of being a trade union – and a radical one at that – warned that its members had had enough. If anything, growers had been *too* loyal, it said in 1923. 'Well, times are changing, and the history of the past two years – with the record of planters ruthlessly thrown out of work and forced with their families to face the streets which led to ruin and starvation . . . – is not likely to be repeated.' The struggle of union against capital, it warned, had now been joined.

Like most agricultural products, rubber was at the mercy of world demand, but what if that demand could somehow be expanded? In February 1927, *The Planter* announced that a bold experiment was underway: in London, a section of New Bridge Street had been repaved using blocks faced with rubber. The blocks – measuring 10 inches by 8½ by 4¼ – consisted of a hard-brick base to which a vulcanized-rubber cap had been added. 'The blocks weigh about 30 pounds each', said the magazine, 'and give great stability when laid. The face of the rubber is moulded with shallow channels running in the direction of the traffic and affords protection against skidding while ensuring a secure foothold for horse traffic.' They had another benefit. According to one industry group, traffic vibration, which the rubber-clad bricks were said to eliminate, was taking a toll on England's bridges and buildings and, 'in many cases, was slowly but surely destroying them'.

The group also persuaded the authorities in Kensington to try rubber-faced blocks, but other boroughs proved more resistant. 'It would appear that it is going to be a long and tedious process to prove to them that rubber will help in solving the problem of vibration in our cities,' the group complained in a letter to *The Times* in 1929.

As *The Planter* pointed out, this was rubber's greatest test – one which, if successful, would not only make Malaya very rich, but transform the industry as well. But it was not to be. The blocks had a tendency to warp, it turned out, and the experiment was quietly abandoned.

In September 1927 there appeared in the *Mail* a letter bearing a startling headline: 'Coolies Flogged to Death.' 'I have heard today', the letter began, 'from a source the reliability of which is quite beyond doubt that many cruelties are perpetrated against Chinese coolies . . . employed [clearing] the jungles of Pahang and Johore.

'These unfortunate "sinkehs" – virtually slaves – are said to be squeezed in every possible way and their life is such a hell that not a few endeavour to abscond. Should one of these unfortunates be recaptured he is brought back . . . says my informant, and then almost invariably flogged to death.

'A high government official whom I asked [about this] said very reasonably that it was impossible to confirm or deny that such things did happen, but personally he thought that such incidents, though not so common as they were in the old days, might be by no means rare today.

'A stricter inquiry into the deaths of coolies stated to have been carried off by tigers or to have died of snake bite or to have met with some other convenient end might well be made. Several years ago, the police in Pahang exhumed the body of a coolie who was alleged to have died of fever and what they found was enlightening, if very horrible.' The letter was signed GRT, presumably G. R. Tonkin, one of the *Mail*'s sub-editors.

Planters often complained that they were ill-used, but Malaya's real victims – the people whose treatment sparked protests both in the FMS and in Britain – were the labourers who toiled on rubber estates. Most of these people were Tamils, a group the British did not especially like. Bruce Lockhart, whose instincts were fairly liberal, objected to what he called their 'pungent odour', while Arthur Keyser – known to his friends as Poppyhead – dismissed them as stupid. No matter how simple a task, he said, a Tamil will always find a way to botch it. Tamils, he claimed, were, and always would be, babies.

Even those who professed to admire Tamils did so condescendingly. One man described them as 'very simple and childlike and the best results are obtained by treating them exactly as Sunday School pupils at home'. Even their women failed to inspire desire. It was said that before he would consider consorting with one, a Briton would have to be very drunk or very desperate.

If the planter saw himself as at the mercy of the visiting agent, his workers were at *his* mercy. One boasted that he knew nothing about the science of growing rubber. He did it all, he said, by 'rule of thump', by which he meant that he drove his workers mercilessly, and when one of them objected, he gave him a thrashing.

When the first issue of *The Planter* appeared in 1920, it contained this chilling piece of doggerel:

If a cooley [sic] gives you cheek
And you can catch the giver
To make him civil heave a brick
And dislocate his liver.
When he refuses labour
Or works in a manner airy
Just knock him down and while he's there
Jump on his little mary.
Any time you find him do
What he didn't oughter
Don't hesitate and shove him in
A boiling pot of water.

Workers were being given notice that if, for any reason, they failed to cooperate, they would suffer for it. And they did. Sometimes grievously. In November 1909, an official visiting an estate near Taiping found '27 coolies . . . showing every evidence of having been maltreated'. One worker, dying of dysentery, was said to have 'attempted to hang himself sooner than put up with the treatment he was receiving'. Another man had been struck fifty-three times 'with a rattan about an inch thick'. The case against the two assistant managers charged with inflicting this abuse was tried before a compliant Malay magistrate who, instead of sending them to prison, fined them a total of $300 – a little less than £40.

Labourers might find themselves punished for anything: for singing Indian songs on Gandhi's birthday; for scowling; for getting drunk; for talking back to a foreman. One man was fined for cycling past the manager's house. (The man did not know it, but he should have dismounted.) On some plantations, workers were kept in a state of near-terror, and there was little they could do about it. They could, of course, run away, and on occasion some of them did, but many estates being remote, there was nowhere they *might* run – unless they took their chances in the jungle.

Some tried this and died of hunger or were eaten by tigers; others were caught and returned to the place they had tried to flee. And then what? Since the fugitive had dared to challenge authority, the planter felt compelled to teach him a lesson. There was a moral here for everyone – not least for those considering flight themselves – and, for this reason, the lesson became a public one, the other workers made to watch while the fugitive was flogged.

The length of the beating – and its severity – depended entirely on the manager's purpose. If he intended it only as a warning, it was short. But if he wanted to instil fear, the victim was thrashed so severely it might be weeks before he could work again. The latter was thought to be more effective because it pressed home not just the power at the manager's disposal, but also the labourers' *lack* of power. More than anything else, the planter liked to say, the Asian respected authority. Fail to be autocratic, and you simply confused him.

Until 1910, there were two kinds of Tamil worker in Malaya. One group bore the title 'free', and the other was indentured. The indenture system was particularly shameful. It emerged in the 1840s, a few years after the Emancipation Bill outlawed slavery. This was no coincidence. Critics of indenture said it was slavery in another guise. Indentured labourers had no rights. By agreeing to work for a specific period – usually three years – they became, in effect, their employer's property.

Indentured labourers were often worked until they were so debilitated that work became impossible. Then they were discarded. Most employers 'undertook to maintain their workers at as small a cost as possible, and to keep them on the job as regularly as possible,' wrote K. S. Sandhu. 'At the end of the indenture, he tried to renew the agreement for another stretch if the worker was still productive, or to get rid of him if he was not.'

After being recruited in India, labourers were shipped to Penang. Most thought they were travelling free. It was never explained to them that the cost of their passage would be deducted from their wages. The labourer, misled into thinking that a fortune awaited him in Malaya, arrived in the country deep in debt. Many were still indebted when their contracts expired, giving them little choice but to sign for another term.

These people earned barely enough to live on. Their wages – 40 to 50 cents a day – shrank to almost nothing when deductions for such things as food and housing had been subtracted. For relief, they turned to loan sharks and compounded their problems. Indentured labourers, poor when they arrived in Malaya, were often destitute when they left. If, that is, they left at all. Many died, cut down by malaria and typhus, cholera and pneumonia, smallpox and tuberculosis.

Workers who fell ill were known as hospital birds, a term intended to suggest that the person claiming sickness was a shirker. This was one reason why people hesitated to see a doctor. Another was this: irrespective of how ill they were, if they didn't work, they weren't paid. In order to go to hospital, a worker needed the permission of his manager, and that permission was not always forthcoming. The planter might decide that the worker was dissembling or that his symptoms were not serious or, because he was short of staff that day, that he could not afford to lose another hand.

In March 1910, an estate manager appeared in court in Kuala Lumpur to answer a charge that he had failed 'to send to hospital an Indian coolie . . . in need of medical treatment'. The labourer had chronic pneumonia and had been ill for over a week. He died nine days later. The case was dismissed.

Labourers lived, sometimes six to a room, in blocks one man described as 'glorified horse boxes'. But planters denied charges that they exploited impoverished and defenceless people. Tamils, they said, earned in Malaya three times what they had in India, where, had they stayed, they would very likely have died of starvation. (They neglected to mention that Malaya was three times as expensive.) When a worker's expenses had been deducted, planters claimed, he had enough every month not only to buy necessities, but to save a little as well.

The *Mail*, which had its blind spots, agreed, contending in September 1910 that workers were not just adequately paid, they had as well 'everything found – even to tobacco and barbers'. Instead of criticizing planters, workers should go down on their knees and thank them. The paper also contended that Tamils had legal protection. Government inspectors, it said, often went to estates 'and any complaint is carefully inquired into'. This was poppycock. Workers did not dare to voice their grievances, knowing full well what would happen if they did. Interviewed in the presence of an assistant manager, they did the sensible thing and kept their mouths shut.

(From 1923, a worker could be fined if a complaint he made was found to be frivolous, though just what constituted frivolity was never made clear. The new labour code of that year also made it illegal for children under ten to work on estates, and it ordered the building of nurseries. Until then, female labourers tapped trees and cleared weed accompanied by their babies.)

With time, the situation eased a little, though not because of any growth of sensitivity. The improvement came in response to international pressure from groups like the Aborigines Protection Society and individuals like Sir Henry Cotton who, in 1907, complained in *The Nation* that the death rate among indentured workers in Malaya was appalling and revealed 'an amount of misery and suffering dreadful to contemplate'.

The *Mail* flew to the attack. Though it did not challenge Cotton's figure of eighty-four deaths per thousand – twice the rate in the general population – it described the British MP as 'a crank who has made himself an unmitigated nuisance' and accused him of suggesting 'that the planters of the FMS are making huge profits by slavery, and that they are employing in the collection of their rubber the same methods which have been employed on the Congo'. The Cotton campaign worked nevertheless. In June 1910, the British government outlawed indentured immigration.

By doing so, London had rid itself of a major embarrassment, but this left 'free' labourers who endured the same awful conditions and who worked for the same dismal pay. What of them? They had a remedy, the government said. Since they were not bound by any contract, they could, if they did not like their jobs, seek work elsewhere. This was true only in theory. A man who wished to change estates had first to get his employer's permission, which was often withheld. Most of the time, though, there was nothing to be gained by seeking other work. Since employers in a region often colluded to keep down wages, workers lacked any real options.

So the abuses continued notwithstanding government claims that safeguards were now in place and that planters had seen the light. As late as 1922, managers were still being accused of flogging workers – charges the *Mail* dismissed as calumnies. 'There are black sheep in every fold,' it said, 'and isolated cases are naturally made much of by propagandists.'

The Labour Department did try from time to time to curtail these abuses, but it found itself stymied, first by planters, who said the department was full of socialists who were out to destroy them; and then by geography. There was simply too much ground to cover, and many officials lost heart, rushing through cursory inspections before hurrying back to the manager's bungalow where a lavish lunch was waiting for them.

There were two factions in the government: those who tended to favour the planters – a majority – and those whose sympathies lay with labour. But an even greater problem was the lack of political will. The government might chide planters from time to time, but it could not afford to make enemies of them. Malaya's cash cow, the rubber industry, generated huge revenues. Without it, the economy would collapse. The government knew this, knew that its interests and planters' interests were one and the same. The government might grouse, but grouse was the size of it. The planters could afford to be obdurate. In the end, they knew they would get their way.

12

The Imp of the Perverse

Tamils were not the only ones to succumb to disease; the British did too, in large numbers. The British felt embattled in Malaya, another reason they hated the place. Its dangers were insidious, impersonal, ubiquitous, dangers that favoured no one – least of all the stewards of empire.

Hailing from the frigid north, the Briton in Malaya felt himself at a grave disadvantage. Not only were there the terrors of malaria and dysentery to contend with, there were the twin horrors of heat and humidity – the first asphyxiating, the second so dense it was easy to imagine yourself wading through egg whites. (Malaya was so humid, Curle tells us, that 'a box of matches left overnight by your bed-side will not strike in the morning'.)

In their new environment, the British felt vulnerable and exposed. And frightened too. They could, if they had to, fight off measles and colds. With the right treatment, they could even survive pneumonia. These were British ailments which fell within the bounds of their experience. But malaria? Blackwater fever? These were new to them. New and very vicious.

Nor could they seek reassurance in science. In the early part of the century, 'miasma theory' was part of the orthodoxy – the notion that disease could not be avoided because it permeated the atmosphere. By this explanation, preventive measures availed one little. One was nature's plaything, hers to dispose of as she pleased.

Some thought this smacked too much of fatalism and turned instead to a set of prescriptions in a booklet called *General Information for Intending Settlers.* Published in 1915, it warned that on no account should anyone under twenty emigrate to Malaya – put simply, the young could not withstand its rigours – and then offered these rules which, if followed religiously, reduced one's chances of sudden death:

- Go to bed and get up early.
- Avoid all excesses in eating and drinking.
- Never go out between the hours of 8 a.m. and 4.30. p.m. without a sun hat.
- When possible, always wear flannel next to the skin.
- Exercise regularly and moderately.
- Change clothes as soon as possible after exercise.
- If doubtful about the purity of drinking water, always see personally that it is boiled and don't take the servant's word for it.
- Avoid bathing in the middle of the day or more than twice a day. In the evening or after exercise, a warm bath is better than a cold one.

Rather an odd set of rules grew up around bathing. Some said regular baths increased the body's resistance; others claimed they had the opposite effect and actually lowered it. There were those who favoured *cold* baths in the belief that they made the skin less sensitive to the sun, and those who dismissed this as nonsense, citing as proof the case of a man who, *en route* to Penang in 1911, died of apoplexy after taking a cold-water bath 'while feeling the effects of the heat'. (The incident occurred in the Red Sea, I would read later in the *Mail*, and 'cast a gloom over the ship'.)

Everyone had his own regimen which he never tired of promulgating. (Those who had been in the country for any length of time were especially free with their advice. Having avoided serious illness for all of two years, they considered themselves survivors.) One man strongly advocated 'the use of shade glasses', being of the opinion that the bright tropic light adversely affected the nerves. Another stressed the importance of sleeping in the afternoon and urged the British 'to follow the example of those in India where the after-tiffin rest is almost universally adopted'. And a third, described as having 'long experience of work in the tropics', advocated four or five glasses of water a day, and plenty of exercise in both the morning and the evening 'when the [sun's] ultra-violet rays are at their maximum'.

It was all of very little help. Starting around 1920 when measures against malaria began to take effect, Malaya became progressively less dangerous. But until then – and especially during the Proudlock years – their health preoccupied the British. There were times, indeed, when they thought of little else, and with good reason. Death came suddenly in Malaya, striking down even the very strongest.

According to records in St Mary's Church, twenty Britons – sixteen adults and four infants – died in KL in 1910, done in, as one writer put it, by 'a climate for which they had not been bred [and] by diseases they would never have known in their native England'. This was not entirely true. The babies died of pneumonia, bronchitis, meningitis and convulsions – all too common in England – and two of the adults suffered heart attacks, but the others met with less familiar deaths: malaria, blackwater fever, dysentery, paralysis, chronic diarrhoea and apoplexy.

What startles most about the adult dead is their comparative youth. The youngest, one of the dysentery cases, was a mere twenty-two and the oldest, felled by a bad heart, had just turned thirty-eight. These people should not have died; they were in their prime.

What frightened the British most were the small things: a cut, a scratch, a bruise. Things that in England could be ignored were, in Malaya, potentially deadly. In March 1927, the *Mail* reported the death in KL of R. B. Francis, a twenty-four-year-old rubber planter who died just a few days after falling off his motorbike. 'His only wound was a small clean cut on the inner side of the right knee about an inch long and an inch deep,' the paper said. A doctor who attended him described the injury as minor. But while in hospital, Francis developed tetanus and, forty-eight hours later, he was dead.

Francis's case was far from isolated. In June 1910, the *Mail* carried news of the death of Charles Finlay, an estate manager who had died of hydrophobia, 'the result of a bite by a puppy some weeks ago'. H. Ashby Mason had to have a leg amputated because of blood poisoning 'which originated in a blister on a toe'. Dudley Felsinger, the father of two small children, met an even worse fate, succumbing in January 1923 to septic poisoning, a consequence, the *Mail* said, of an abscess on his right hand.

Some of the reports are heartbreaking. Felsinger, as well as caring for two children, was supporting a sick mother in Ceylon; Alfred Potts, employed in the Public Works Department, left a wife he had married just a year and a half earlier; and then there was Leonard Attfield, killed by blackwater fever and eulogized in the *Mail* as 'naturally shy and reserved, honest and trustworthy – the type of planter that would in every way uphold the best traditions of his profession'. Death carried off the best and the brightest, people like H. T. B. Crapper, who died after eating contaminated meat. 'He had demonstrated great ability in the direction of classics and literature and had written a number of clever poems,' the *Mail* reported. His early demise 'is deeply regretted'.

Some people did not last long in Malaya. In December 1910, Kenneth Thorpe succumbed to malaria after being there a mere six weeks. Frank Dent didn't fare much better. When he died – another malaria victim – he had lived in Malaya all of ten months. R. Latham survived eleven-and-a-half months. In January 1911, he was carried off by dysentery. His death caught his friends off guard. They had been planning a party for him. He had just turned twenty-one.

According to his doctor, Latham might have survived but for a recent bout of measles, but it was sending him to Penang's General Hospital that sealed his fate. Woefully primitive and dangerously understaffed, it was so feared that people consented to go there only as a last resort. In August 1910, just months before Latham died, the *Straits Echo* complained that conditions, already deplorable, got ever worse: 'The cubicles are still illuminated by dangerous oil lamps [and] the bells are out of order. Patients are sometimes left quite a long time without the means of summoning help.'

The hospital was also rat-infested – but then so was much of Malaya. As late as November 1922, a fatal case of plague occurred in KL, the government warning people to steer clear of dead rodents. By then, KL was long accustomed to public-health emergencies. In 1910 alone, there were three of them. In January, there were calls for a quarantine when Taiping and Penang both reported outbreaks of smallpox. In August, there was a sharp increase in malaria cases (thirty-nine malaria deaths were recorded in June, fifty-three in August, and sixty in September). In November, two cases of leprosy were reported.

Leprosy was considered enough of a threat that KL had its own leprosy asylum, though the amount of asylum it afforded seems to have been negligible. The place was run with little supervision, and inmates came and went at will. In 1909, one inmate was discovered not far from the Spotted Dog selling chickens. In January 1922, conditions had worsened, the lepers complaining that they were cold at night and were not being given sufficient food. The government took immediate action, though not to address these shortcomings. It had the lepers arrested and charged them with unruly behaviour.

For years, Malaya's primary killer was malaria. By one estimate, it was responsible for 200,000 deaths in the FMS between 1908 and 1919, and almost as many again in the 1920s, when the population was considerably larger. Some of these deaths could doubtless have been avoided had not so many thought of malaria as a fact of life. Just before the onset of the First World War, scientists made two important advances: first, the species of mosquito that carries malaria was identified; and then a compound was developed that, sprayed on drains and other areas where mosquitoes laid their eggs, deprived the larvae of oxygen and prevented them from hatching. But as late as 1923, *The Planter* was insisting that 'all has been done that can . . . be done. Malaria . . . cannot be prevented and must therefore be endured.'

Mosquitoes were a menace. People spent their evenings, fly swat in hand, leaping round their living rooms, slapping wildly, whirling, lashing out – a *danse macabre* that made them look like disciples of Isadora Duncan. At night, they slept in beds cocooned in yards and yards of netting. If, that is, they were *able* to sleep. Many, like Winstedt, lay awake and 'listened to the battle cry of the oncoming horde that flung their diaphanous bodies against the netting' and felt 'those hundreds of microscopic eyes focused avidly on white skin'. When, as often happened, Winstedt's netting proved inadequate, that able gentleman was prepared, wire-flap at the ready, his feet and legs tightly wrapped, his arms smeared with citronella oil and, in his mouth, 'the foulest brand of Burmese cheroot'. If those measures did not work, there was to hand the ultimate weapon: a box of matches. 'When all one's redoubts have fallen, one may still pursue individual enemies with a lighted match . . . If one's sight is abnormally keen and one's hand quick beyond the ordinary, then the enemy is singed and explodes with a pop and dies.'

Malaria nearly killed Winstedt. Shortly after contracting it, he developed blood poisoning which later became acute septicemia. In all, he spent six months in hospital and underwent surgery twenty-two times. 'I was now continuously in greater pain than I have ever suffered even when a tooth was being extracted without an anaesthetic.' For much of that six-month period, he lived on milk and soda. Twelve stone when he entered hospital, he weighed half that when he left. For years afterwards, his malaria would return occasionally. It was only when he started drinking a bottle of claret with every meal that it ceased entirely.

Lockhart, by contrast, treated *his* malaria with brandy flips. The disease struck hard at him as well ('my clothes hung in loose folds on my wasted frame') and left him with a bad heart, an enlarged liver, a defective spleen and a 'ruined' digestion.

One of Winstedt's doctors was a man called Dowden whose father was the distinguished Dublin Shakespearean scholar. So many of Dowden's patients had malaria, he devised what he called the 'injection tea'. Once a week, as many as half a dozen men converged on the doctor's house where, after eating cake and sandwiches, they lowered their trousers, presented their bottoms and received a shot of quinine. It worked out very well for Dowden. It cut down on his house calls.

Terrified of infection, the British were proper tigers when it came to hygiene, which is why KL's produce market so exercised them. One man writing in 1927 said he hated to go there because, everywhere you looked, 'coolies' were spitting. He had once seen a lorry-load of fish unloaded on to 'a filthy muddy floor'. The fish was later washed, he admitted, but even so, 'it was not an appetizing sight'.

Three months later, the market was taken to task again – this time in a letter to the *Mail*. Why, the writer wanted to know, were 'not-clean-looking' servants allowed to pick through loaves of bread until they found one they happened to like. 'It is quite within the realm of possibility that one or more of them suffered from skin disease, syphilis or even leprosy,' he wrote. 'It is not pleasant to think of, but later in the day some of these loaves after being freely handled appear on our tables.'

The British regarded servants as the enemy within. They were the agents of contagion who had breached their walls and bred pestilence in their living rooms. Dhobies, they believed, infected their linens, cooks contaminated their food, and amahs gave off vapours that imperilled their children. Servants, they complained, did not bathe as much as *they* did. (Probably true. But then they did not have to; they had adapted to the climate.) And questions were raised about their other habits – their endless hacking, for example, and the vigour with which they spat. The British so disapproved of spitting, they once tried to bar the Chinese – who take their spitting seriously – from first-class railway carriages. (There were other reasons, too. Chinese men removed their shoes when they took their seats, and they shouted to one another – not unreasonable on a moving train. How else could one hope to make oneself heard?)

William Steward hated spitters, according to Mrs Proudlock. Because it was raining on the night of the murder, Ethel had suggested letting the rickshaw puller wait in the kitchen. But Steward would have none of it – he did not care to hear him spit – and ordered the man to wait in the street. G. L. Peet hated spitters, too, threatening his servants with dismissal if they coughed, sneezed, hacked or spat anywhere near him and going so far as to give each of them handkerchiefs – at his own expense, he was quick to tell his readers. No more, he said, would a civilized household witness practices more appropriate to the Middle Ages.

While many Britons experienced health problems in Malaya, not all of them were caused by tropical diseases. The British diet must bear some of the blame. Breakfasts were large, lunches were huge and then, after a short hiatus, the marathon resumed: afternoon tea at four, drinks at the club at six, and at nine, a monstrous dinner after which, fully gorged, the Briton was led away to bed.

The British ate far too much, the *Mail* warned, and many men, even if they did not know it, were martyrs to indigestion. 'It is no wonder', the paper said in 1927, 'that many young men after a year in Malaya have lost the clear skin and bright eyes with which they came from England.' Indigestion, the *Mail* warned, led inevitably to over-drinking. 'Depressed and irritable, they take the advice of the older men and try a stengah or a gin pahit to cheer themselves up' and in no time became alcoholics.

Much over-drinking was caused by neurasthenia, a nervous disorder which the *Mail* described as rusting minds almost as swiftly as it rusted iron. Slowly wearing the sufferer down, neurasthenia manifested itself in myriad ways. The victim had trouble concentrating; he tired easily; he became lethargic; he grew irritable and depressed. Even more alarming, he lost his sense of purpose. A serious development, this. Ostensibly at least, the British were in Malaya to further the aims of empire. Lollygagging simply wouldn't do.

What caused neurasthenia? One man blamed the absence of winds, another tedium. Sidney thought anxiety the culprit. 'What wears one out', he said, 'is not hard work, but the mental worry which may have no connection with work at all.' According to Curle, it was the fault of Malaya's verdure. 'It is the greenest country on earth,' he wrote, 'and the nervous exhaustion caused by Malaya may be partially explained by her green monotony.' Related to this was another reason: a growing sense of alienation. 'The longer one lives in the tropics, the clearer one sees their complete divorce from one's inward idea of home. For the idea of home is rest, and the note of the tropics is unrest in the ferment of their growth beneath the aching sun.' (Curle much admired Conrad and at times tried to sound like him, though never with much success.)

This was closer to the mark. The British hated the sun and hated the heat, and if they drank too freely, it may only have been to desensitize themselves to the ravages of both. The heat, one man said, put him in mind of a furnace or a battery of searchlights, their beams trained on you all at once. It was also unrelenting. Malaya did not have seasons. The country was hot year-round. It was hot even when the sun went down. It was a battle just to get to sleep. Some went to bed wrapped in wet sheets and others resorted to 'Dutch widows' – a long, bolster-like object which, Leopold Ainsworth tells us, afforded 'great comfort when used in the proper way which is to place it between one's legs in order to keep them apart to allow air to pass between them, for the humid heat is so great that if one's legs touch each other, they perspire profusely'.

Neurasthenia could strike anyone, Dr S. C. Howard wrote in 1933. 'I have seen lusty looking youngsters in their early twenties . . . evince many symptoms of early neurasthenia after only three and a half years in this country.' The end result, Howard went on, 'is a considerably lowered standard of efficiency and a tendency to procrastination, alcoholism, and a definite general weakening of the moral fibre which may culminate in depression, mental breakdown and suicide.'

The word suicide occurs often in the literature about this country. There can be few groups anywhere who killed themselves as much as the British did. The suicide rate in Malaya far exceeded that in England, and during those times when the economy was in recession, it positively soared. In the Straits Settlements in 1930 the suicide rate stood at 9.41 per thousand. In 1931, it jumped to 34.73 per thousand. And in 1932, it jumped again, this time to 94.76. Even allowing for bad times, the increase is staggering. In the early 1930s, England, too, was in recession, but its suicide rate changed hardly at all.

The British killed themselves at the drop of a hat. Sometimes they had cause, as when, in 1938, John Newbold, a Penang businessman, took poison after the plane he was landing struck a car and killed three of its occupants. But more often, people did themselves in on the flimsiest of pretexts – when they were jilted or lost their jobs or were passed over for promotion. One man hanged himself, using a towel hitched to a door, because his leave was cancelled. Even tough old Winstedt gave serious thought to ending it all. Depressed to discover that as a consequence of all that time in bed his legs had atrophied, he felt, he said, 'like returning my life-ticket to the power that gave it'. And he would have, too, he assures us, had he just been able to find a gun.

Not a year went by, the Bishop of Singapore wrote in 1926, but one or more officials went mad or took their own lives. In one recent six-month period, he said, two senior officials had had nervous breakdowns, and two others, occupying 'positions of great honour', had shot themselves. Suicide was even more common among non-officials. John Robson, the well-liked managing director of the *Malay Mail*, knew personally ten men who killed themselves. Women were much more staunch, apparently. He could recall only one instance of a British female committing suicide. She did so quietly, drowning herself in a bath tub while, in the next room, servants set the table for lunch.

While most suicides put guns to their heads, others cut their throats, slashed their wrists or took poison. In February 1911, a clerk in Singapore died 'in great agony' after ingesting carbolic acid. Eight months later, a planter swallowed opium dissolved in a glass of water. The man had been battling white ants, the *Mail* said, and was much run down. Before downing the fatal draught, he posted a cheque to Penang, renewing his life insurance.

Not all intending suicides were successful. In 1921, a 'boy' employed in an Ipoh hotel found a planter 'with his throat cut and staggering about the room in a semi-conscious condition', said the *Mail*. 'The windpipe was cut, but fortunately the arteries were not severed, and it is believed that the victim will recover.' The planter was out of work and had come to Ipoh in hopes of finding a job.

The *Mail* blamed Malaya's suicide rate on an impulse that can seize a man when he is mentally exhausted, an impulse it called the imp of the perverse. 'This wanton devil', the paper said in 1927, 'comes suddenly and is limited to a few seconds. Resist it for a minute and the danger is over. But if you are caught unawares . . . you may kill yourself unwillingly.' For those the imp *did* catch off guard, the paper had some curious advice. 'The best mind-steadier in these crucial moments is to repeat to yourself a multiplication table or one of Euclid's propositions.'

I doubt if even Euclid could have saved Arthur Julius Weller, one of Malaya's top educators. When Weller died of a gunshot wound to the head on 5 October 1922, he had been quietly desperate for almost a year. In a letter found near his body, Weller explained what it was that had driven him to kill himself. 'Dear Wolff,' it began. (E. C. H. Wolff was Weller's superior.) 'Influenza in November, the death of my son in December, the collapse of my wife's health in the early part of the year, the fear that she would commit suicide on her way home [to England], the difficulties with my trustees, the rumours of retrenchment, the strain of the work, the need for a real holiday and inability to take one, the recurrence of flu in August, the knowledge that I am unsuited for my job, the effort to stick to my work when I was harassed to death by my own affairs, the knowledge that I never committed a greater error than I did when I accepted this appointment and that my son's death and my wife's collapse are due to this error . . . All these things combined to wear me out till my nerves and brain are gone. I have really been unfit for work for weeks, but I have struggled on in the belief that I might yet turn failure into success and prove the truth of Kipling's "If". But I cannot go on any longer. Thank you for your kindness and forgive me if you can.' It was signed, 'Yours sincerely, A. J. Weller.'

It was revealed at the inquest that Weller was overdrawn at the bank and had hoped to pay off his overdraft by persuading his wife to sell her securities. After agreeing to do so, she changed her mind and returned to England where she bought a house, the bill for which was sent to her insolvent husband.

In the several months since, she had written to him again and again to reproach him for what she said was the cruel way he had treated her.

At the time of his death, Weller was sharing a house with C. G. Coleman, once a colleague of William Proudlock's. (Coleman had done well for himself. He was now Inspector of Schools, Selangor.) Weller's son had been two years old when the boy fell ill and died, Coleman told the inquest. The death occurred when Weller was away in Perak, and the fear that he had failed the boy preyed on the dead man's sanity. Weller, Coleman finished, was an excellent civil servant and was widely respected. The court returned a verdict of suicide while temporarily insane.

Neurasthenia does not entirely explain Malaya's suicide rate. Conditions in Malaya and in the neighbouring Dutch East Indies were very similar. Why then did the Dutch not kill themselves as promiscuously as the British did? Why did the sun not rust *their* minds?

While the Dutch had their faults, some of them major, they proved more adaptable than the British. Having left Holland, they did not make a fetish of nostalgia. Not being as culturally rigid, they did not isolate themselves. They adopted local dress, ate local foods, took local mistresses and spoke at least one local language. And they had interests. 'The Dutchman talks of language, history, music, art,' Winstedt said. 'The Englishman, playing for safety . . . talks of games and horses.' The Dutch, in short, made the best of things. The British did not. For many of them, their lives in Malaya were joyless and constrained – enough to drive anyone to suicide. There was something else as well. The British did not kill themselves only because they had failed; they killed themselves because they were not supposed to fail. What proved their undoing was their own hyperbole. If the Briton was all-capable, why was he not able to rout those white ants? If he took everything in his stride, why was it that he could not cope? If he was self-sufficient, why did he feel so lonely? What did that mean? Just this: that he was a very poor specimen indeed; a Briton not deserving of the name.

13

A Tory Eden

One of the advantages of living in KL, a government handbook said, is that 'it does not require the European or the Asiatic to live side by side'. This was not just the case in the FMS capital; there was very little contact between the races anywhere in Malaya.

One woman complained that, after a decade in the FMS, she knew no more about Asians than she had when she arrived. 'One feels as much of a stranger in the Selangor coastal plain', she wrote, 'as one does in Italy when one travels through the Italian vineyards and olive groves to see Pompeii.'

This separation of the races 'is perhaps the most significant part of our life in this country,' said G. L. Peet. 'We all live in compartments and only occasionally do we scramble over the dividing walls.' How could it be otherwise? he wanted to know. Except for civil servants, few Britons spoke Malay and even fewer knew the first thing about Chinese. Before they could mix socially, the races would first have to share a common language. In this regard, though, Peet offended as much as anyone. Although he had been living in KL for years, his Malay, he admitted, was atrocious – limited, as he put it, 'to crude domestic necessities'.

Others, though, did not envisage a crash course in languages helping very much. The racial divide could never be bridged, they said, because the attitudes of the Asian and the Briton were at such odds as to rule out any understanding. Sidney was warned by an old Malaya hand that 'you will never probe beneath the Asiatic mask, nor get down to their mind. They will pretend to fall in with your projects, but as soon as your back is turned. . .'

Most Britons approved of racial separation. The twain did not have to meet; it was enough that they collaborate. Malaya was proof that Platonism worked, the *Mail* said in July 1927. The Malays were happy; the Indians were happy; and as long as you let them make money, the Chinese were happy, too. Even the British, by God, were happy, having realized 'that, so long as you can be sure of its benevolence, a benevolent autocracy such as rules this country is in practice quite the best form of government for the east'.

The picture this paints of Malaya as a racial Shangri-la is misleading. The British disliked the Chinese, the Chinese disliked the Malays, and the Malays, at one time or another, seem to have disliked everyone. A failure of British policy, one is tempted to think. But this was not the case. It *was* British policy – that perennial stand-by, divide and rule. While the Malays and the Chinese had always been wary of one another, the British, because it suited their designs, made a bad situation worse. Carefully exploiting Malay fears, they gave them to understand that the Chinese opposed their progress, and that, were the British to leave, the Malays would find themselves stripped of their birthright.

The British claimed to like Malays, largely for the reason that they kept their distance. According to one official, one could share a hut with a Malay and not worry about being dug in the ribs or being called by one's Christian name. But by 1911, the day when a Briton *might* have shared a hut with a Malay was long gone. The government had been centralized now and supporting it was a civil service whose requirements meant that district officers no longer had time to venture from their desks.

The Chinese were another matter. The British had no time for them. When the Chinese rioted in KL in 1912, one man proposed shooting them down like dogs. This hostility took many forms, one of which was sometimes pretending that the Chinese did not exist. When KL was flooded in 1926, several Chinese drowned and hundreds more lost their homes. The newspapers largely ignored this, stressing instead the hardships that the British endured: 'For nine days, three English ladies and two children lived in the railway engineer's [bungalow] without mosquito nets.'

The British complained that the Chinese were truculent. (One man was greatly taken aback when a Chinese he had pushed turned around and *glared* at him.) Even worse in British eyes, they did not know their place – another way of saying they refused to be obsequious. The British had come to expect obeisance. Show them anything less and they thought it insolence. The Chinese refused to kowtow (a Chinese word, incidentally). Indians bowed and scraped when the British entered their shops. The Chinese let them wait. Indians yielded their seats on trains. The Chinese let them stand. They were every bit as good as the British, maybe even better.

In Maugham's play *East of Suez*, George, a civil servant, tells Lee Tai, a wealthy businessman, that if he loves China, he will 'accept honestly and sincerely the teaching of the West'. But what if we despise what the West has to teach us? Lee wants to know. 'For what reason are you so confident that you are superior to us that it behooves us to sit humbly at your feet? Have you excelled us in arts and letters? Have our thinkers been less profound than yours? Has our civilization been less elaborate, less complicated, less refined than yours? Why, when you lived in caves and clothed yourselves with skins we were a cultured people.'

When it came to claims of racial superiority, the Chinese and the British were evenly matched. E. N. T. Cummins, a well-known KL planter, learned this the hard way. In 1927, Cummins ordered a fourteen-year-old Chinese boy out of his way, but instead of meekly stepping aside, the boy said, 'Who do you think you are?' When Cummins recovered himself, he struck the boy so hard in the face, he made his nose bleed. In court, Cummins said he would not have hit the child if he had known he was fourteen. He was under the impression he was fifteen. The magistrate took the view that Cummins had been provoked and, with much reluctance, fined the planter the token sum of $25.

While it is true that the British never much liked the Chinese, in the early days they did at least show them respect. That ended when Dr James Barrack was murdered. Barrack met his end on 15 July 1908, when several Chinese ambushed him and another Englishman on a lonely jungle road in Pahang. Their intended target had been Barrack's companion, an unscrupulous contractor named Gregor MacLean who had swindled them out of money. Because MacLean fled when the Chinese broke cover, they vented their rage on Barrack instead. Barrack raised his hands and called out something in English, but it didn't help. When he was found an hour later, he was lying on the road with his arms outstretched and his hands clenched, a knife protruding from his throat.

Nine people – one of them a woman – were charged with his murder. This is how the *Mail* described the scene when the case came to trial some three months later: 'The little court was crowded with diverse nationalities. In the midst of this crowd, guarded by stalwart sikhs, sat the prisoners mostly in attitudes suggesting apathy or indifference. Outside, a violent thunder storm raged, but inside in the semi-darkness, a lamp lit up the scarlet robes of the judicial commissioner.'

Several irregularities attended this trial, as they would Mrs Proudlock's. The murder provoked an outcry, and the authorities went all out to secure a conviction. At least three defendants were pressured into signing confessions, witnesses were paid for their testimony, and during the trail Mr Justice Braddell referred to the defendants again and again as ruffians. The police arrested people at will. One man was taken into custody because he had a hat similar to one owned by Barrack, and another because he trembled when a policeman asked him a question. While awaiting trial, one of the accused tried to hang himself. He was innocent, he said, and rather than let the authorities kill him, he preferred to do the job himself.

Eight of the nine were sentenced to hang. When the verdict was read, the judge 'assumed the black cap and passed sentence on the prisoners, remarking that it would be a waste of words to say anything to the crude ruffians who had committed such a terrible crime. The prisoners for the most part received the death sentences with outward indifference.' Four of the death sentences were later commuted to life in prison.

The Barrack case galvanized Malaya. He was an innocent victim, yes, but there was more involved. His death struck deep because for the first time 'one of us' had met a horrible end at the hands of 'one of them'. Barrack's death made everyone feel vulnerable and, because of it, the general unease with which the Chinese had been regarded crystallized now into out-and-out fear. They were different. They were deadly. They had to be watched.

Over the next several years, letters to the *Mail* took on an increasingly strident anti-Chinese tone. There were the familiar complaints about their hygiene and their honesty, and some new ones as well, having to do with their motives and their loyalty to the crown. Even their language came in for criticism. They did not speak, it was said, they clamoured in that awful Cantonese. There was nothing about the Chinese that someone did not find objectionable. There were demands that their activities be regulated, that the clan houses come in for greater scrutiny, that the authorities suppress the Chinese passion for gambling.

In 1912, the government did ban gambling briefly and the results were disastrous: nearly a week of rioting that caused twelve deaths, brought much of KL to a standstill and so shook British confidence that any lingering affection for the Chinese now disappeared for ever. The reason for the ban is not completely clear. The Chinese had been gambling ever since arriving in Malaya, so it could not be argued that wagering posed a threat. And to impose a ban just then – at the start of Chinese New Year, a major festival – makes it even more inexplicable. The intention may have been to punish the Chinese, or the authorities may simply have been feeling insecure. Malaya was still getting over the Proudlock trial, and the government may have wanted to make a point: its credibility had perhaps been damaged, but it remained, for all that, securely in control. Whatever the reason, the decision proved fatal. Unable to gamble and at a loss for something to do, Chinese factions fell to fighting one another. Within hours, pitched battles were being waged all over Chinatown.

The fighting caught the government completely off guard. Scrambling, the authorities placed KL on something like a general alert. Two companies of the Malay States Guides were dispatched from Taiping; the Malay States Volunteer Rifles were mobilized; and to prevent arms reaching the rioters, all trains entering the city were searched. Saying that they needed to protect themselves, some twenty Britons marched to the armoury and demanded rifles. The government refused and ordered the men back to their homes.

One observer described the Chinese as conducting a reign of terror. This was to exaggerate, but there is no question that, for a time, the British lost control of a large section of the city. Mobs roamed where they pleased. Houses were put to the torch. Shops were looted. Policemen were kicked and punched. And then, on Day 4, the tide turned. That morning, a crowd armed with stones and bottles entered Sultan Street and tried to storm the police station. The police fixed bayonets and drove the crowd back. Again it charged, and again it was repulsed. When it attacked for a third time, the police opened fire, and several Chinese fell dead. Less than twenty-four hours later, KL was quiet for the first time in almost a week.

As was their wont in these situations, the British made light of the riots. A purely Chinese affair, they said; at no point had *they* been threatened. Which was not to say that they had not been inconvenienced. For five days, there had been no rickshaws. To get to the club, many had had to walk. But this was mere theatre; an attempt at *sang froid*. The riots seriously rattled the British. People used to joke about the Chinese rising up and cutting their throats. Now it seemed a very real possibility. In the months that followed, there were calls for greater security and for more police. Criticism of the Chinese intensified. They were ungrateful, the British said. They forgot that everything they had, the British had given them; everything they now enjoyed – rising living standards, the rule of law, the freedom to amass great wealth – all this and more they owed to British rule.

This was less than fair. Were it not for Chinese diligence

and Chinese enterprise – to say nothing of the substantial revenues they generated – Malaya would have few of the amenities many now took for granted: roads, railways, electricity and the telephone. But the criticism continued, becoming so vitriolic that the *Mail* finally felt compelled to set the record straight. Were it not for the Chinese, it said, Malaya would still be a backwater. 'The Europeans . . . have been the brain, the guiding and impelling force' in Malaya's development, but they never could have done it unassisted. 'British Malaya is in the main the product of British initiative and Chinese labour. The Chinese can claim no small share of the credit for creating British Malaya as it exists today.'

Harry Foster, an American journalist, put it more succinctly. 'If it were not for the Chinks,' he said, 'this peninsula wouldn't be worth a cent. The Malays won't work any more than the Siamese.'

Most of the Chinese in Malaya were at a disadvantage. Having entered the country on short-term contracts, those who stayed did so at the government's pleasure and could be ordered back to China at a moment's notice. In October 1909, when rickshaw pullers went on strike, the Resident assembled their leaders and told them 'they were aliens here and only allowed in the country . . . as long as they behaved themselves'. The men were then given an ultimatum: if by six that evening the strike had not been called off, every one of them would be deported. An hour later, the rickshaws were back on the streets.

The Banishment Enactment gave the government wide discretion. In December 1908, the *Mail* reported that 'three more "undesirables" have left the country for the country's good'. A month later, forty-three people were banished, four of them German Jews, the rest Chinese. That same month, the British announced a measure to make banishment more humane. Starting immediately, all persons being expelled from the FMS would be provided by the superintendent of prisons with a suit of clothes and a blanket.

What was not humane was the manner in which the law was applied. One man was ordered back to China because, it was said, he had impugned the crown, when all he had really done was to talk back to a British official. The incident occurred in Ipoh in 1909 and involved H. C. Ridges, the protector of Chinese, and Leung Wah Yu. Ridges had asked Leung to write his name in Chinese, and when Leung said, 'Would you be able to read it if I did?', Ridges accused him of insulting a servant of His Majesty. Leung was then arrested, placed in shackles, removed to prison and, in the fullness of time, sentenced to five years' banishment.

In Britain, many saw the action as high-handed. In the House of Commons, the Under-secretary of State for the Colonies was asked if he did not think the sentence disproportionate, especially since, a few days earlier, an Englishman in Ipoh had been fined just $75 'for having killed a China man'. The Under-secretary replied that he could not comment as he had still to be briefed on the matter. A second question having to do with whether or not the Colonial Office would now take steps to ensure that all Malaya's races were treated equally was ignored.

In Malaya, the uproar forced a change of heart. Deeply embarrassed, the authorities offered Leung a deal: if he agreed to state publicly that it had not been his intention to insult the British government, the deportation order would be rescinded and he could, if he chose to, remain in the country. The *Mail* applauded the decision, saying that Leung had been guilty of nothing more than impertinence.

The British were fond of saying that if their rule was not always kind, it was never less than just. British law was applied impartialy and favoured no one, neither the rulers nor the ruled. This was twaddle. All Malaya's races were not equal before the law, as the Chinese, many of whom remembered the Barrack trial, knew only too well.

When the British appeared in court, they almost always got the benefit of the doubt, while fifteen-year-old Chinese boys were caned or sent to prison for stealing a packet of cigarettes. The British assaulted people or embezzled large sums of money, and the courts went out of their way to be lenient.

In 1925, Walter Williamson, an English prison guard charged with causing the death of an inmate, pleaded provocation. Williamson told the court that the inmate had made 'an indecent remark'. For this, he had kicked the man so hard, the prisoner's spleen was ruptured. Williamson was sentenced to a month in gaol.

In 1910, a man identified only as 'a well-known European' living in Singapore was charged with attempted murder after firing three times into a crowd of Malays. In court, the deputy public prosecutor, sounding more like the man's lawyer, said the defendant was drunk when the incident occurred and thought the Malays were making fun of him. The man's character was excellent, the prosecutor went on, and he could only imagine that he had acted as he had because of a mild case of sunstroke. The judge accepted this preposterous argument and fined the 'well-known European' $50.

Also in 1910, an Englishman who fled to Sarawak after passing worthless cheques did not simply have the charges against him dropped, he was hailed as a man of rare integrity. The Singapore police ordered a manhunt when P. A. G. Grimes went missing, making it unlikely he would have been at large for long. Grimes would have known this and, quite sensibly, returned to Singapore to turn himself in. He wanted, he said, 'to square things up'. According to the *Mail*, 'the police were *amazed* [my italics] that Grimes had returned of his own free will'. And even more amazing, 'he made no attempt whatever to conceal his identity'. The magistrate decided that no fraud was intended, and Grimes left the court a free man.

The Chinese the British liked least were the rickshaw pullers. 'The coolie who pulls the rickshaw is about the most unpleasant scoundrel who ever came out of the underworld of Canton,' Arthur Keyser wrote. With his copper-coloured skin, his blue shorts, and his wide-brimmed hat, he looks picturesque, Keyser went on, 'but there his beauty ends. He is an inveterate gambler and opium smoker with one aim and object in life: to make money by fair or foul means. He is surly and hates work.'

The British, used to having the upper hand, had a particular fear of rickshaws. The moment they stepped into one, they were at the puller's mercy and, for many, the loss of control was unnerving. The puller was in charge now, and he used the opportunity, the British said, not just to avenge every wrong he had suffered at their hands, but to avenge as well every wrong done to every member of his race.

'When the coolie picks up the shafts,' Keyser said, 'he will do so with a jerk which will throw you back violently, hitting your back against the upright part behind the seat, and as you jog along this will be a constant source of discomfort.' Or the puller might decide that he needed a rest and, with no warning, the shafts would be lowered. When this happened, it was all that a passenger could do to stop himself from pitching forwards and measuring his length along the road.

There were other devices at the puller's disposal. He took corners too quickly, ignored pleas to reduce his speed, and ran with his head down – often on the wrong side of the road. When he reached his destination (by the most circuitous route possible), there was always a fuss about the fare. Words were exchanged, and threats were made. One man said his puller was 'so cheeky', he was tempted to teach him a lesson. But in the end one paid up because there was little one could do except call the police, and that was self-defeating because the puller would tell his colleagues – KL was a small place; it did not take long for word to get around – and the next time one wanted a rickshaw, the pullers would pretend not to notice or claim to be engaged.

Rickshaws were not always clean. In addition to passengers, they were used to transport all sorts of things: vegetables, livestock, hog wash, manures of one kind or another, and what one man called 'abominations too awful to detail'. They also raised moral questions. It was unsettling to be hauled about by another human being, to treat a man as if he were a beast of burden. It was wrong, very wrong, to affront another's dignity like this. People were entitled to respect.

'It seems almost inhuman to be pulled through the streets by a fellow-man,' Richard Sidney said. 'This is more particularly so if your puller happens to be old and somewhat tired.' George Bilainkin found the experience equally disconcerting. 'The master was on the throne,' he said, 'and the slave was in harness . . . I half shut and then opened my eyes and saw the perspiration on the back of the man's vest. It was I who caused this perspiration . . . It seemed a crime to use him thus, and a needless crime.'

Such scruples did not last for long. 'The feeling of humanity very soon leaves one and the taking of a rickshaw becomes an ordinary event,' Sidney said. Sidney stifled his misgivings, but others had no misgivings to stifle. 'These coolies,' wrote Curle, 'have a lollop like an undisturbed hare making for a hedge-gap in the twilight, and they seem able to keep it up indefinitely.'

Actually, they were not. Hauling a rickshaw was gruelling work, and many pullers died young, worn out before their time. Few pulled rickshaws voluntarily. For most, it was a last resort. (Several of Singapore's pullers were out-of-work actors.) Many pullers were ravaged by malaria, and many others were emaciated, reduced by opium to skin and bone.

Towards the Malays, the British were better disposed. In England, Malays were thought to be piratical and fierce and armed to the teeth but, as F. W. Knocker explained, that was before they'd been 'smoothed out and turned aside into Elysian paths by a considerate and parental British government'. Thanks to the British, 'every Malay is a gentleman', said Horace Bleackley, 'even those of the lower orders'. The *Mail* agreed, claiming that of all Asians, Malays are 'the one race with which the Englishman finds it easiest to get on'.

Gentlemen they might be, but it was also said of them that they did not prize exertion. Unless one stood over a Malay 'with a revolver, he will botch and bungle every single job his hand is turned to, and take a wicked pride in it', Ashley Gibson wrote. His tone, though, is indulgent. For all their Protestant fervour where work was concerned, the British looked kindly on the Malays' lack of vigour. Besides, there was something aristocratic about him. He had charm, tact, and exquisite manners. The Malay, the British said, was a splendid fellow. In many ways, a lot like themselves.

If the British liked the Malays, however, there is some evidence that Malays did not always like the British. Soccer matches between the all-British Casuals and the all-Malay Sultan Suleiman Club often ended in fisticuffs, with Malays on the sidelines urging their countrymen on the field to 'kill them' and to 'break their bones'. (This 'unsporting savagery', the *Mail* contended, 'recalls Millwall at its worst'.) By no measure does it suggest racial harmony, but the British refused to be dissuaded; Malaya, they insisted, was a racial paradigm, 'a Tory Eden in which each man is contented with his station and does not wish for change'.

The great mass of Malays gained little from British rule. Even as the economy expanded and investors grew rich, their living standards changed hardly at all, in part because only one child in three received any education. Schooling, said one official, would give Malays ideas above their station and spoil them for manual labour – presumably the one thing for which he thought them suited. The British encouraged Malays to stay in their villages and do as their forebears had done: to farm and to fish.

Those the British presence benefited most were Malaya's sultans. The British provided the native rulers with pensions and stability. The threat of British force put an end to the territorial disputes and wars of succession that had plagued Malaya for much of its history. As long as their wealth and perquisites were left intact, the sultans did not mind sharing power. Many, indeed, were glad to. Now they could devote themselves to polo.

The relationship was a symbiotic one. The sultans needed the British if they were to stay in power, and the British needed the sultans to lend their rule a semblance of legitimacy. Both parties understood they were mutually dependent and for that reason frictions were kept to a minimum. Frictions, though, did occur. A sultan opposed to some new initiative requiring his endorsement would often prevaricate. There were several ways he might do this. He could plead for more time, 'lose' crucial documents, expound upon the dangers of acting hastily, miss meetings, feign illness, take it into his head to visit a neighbouring sultan, or have a neighbouring sultan visit him. The possibilities were endless. Of course, he could not stall indefinitely and, in the end, he did as he was told. But even then, his recalcitrance had served a purpose. The British had been reminded that he was not to be taken for granted; that once in a while, they would have to compromise.

British rule was never seriously challenged, largely for the reason that Britain was very much the *force majeure.* Malays, most of whom lived in small villages along the country's coasts and rivers, were pragmatic enough to know that they could not challenge the Royal Navy, not when its gunboats patrolled the waterways and its warships kept watch at sea.

Even with the odds against them, however, Malays did rise up from time to time. In 1915, farmers in the northern state of Kelantan, protesting a land tax, torched European bungalows and looted the home of a district officer. Leading the uprising was To' Janggut who would not rest, he said, until every white man had been driven from the state. The insurgency faltered when HMS *Cadmus* arrived and trained its guns on Kelantan's capital. When To' Janggut was killed soon afterwards, the British gave orders that his body be suspended by the feet from a lamp post.

Thirteen years later, there was another rebellion, this one in the neighbouring state of Trengganu, its goal the same as the earlier one: to rid the state of the British scourge. Warned that all the Europeans in Kuala Trengganu, the capital, were in danger of being murdered, H. P. Bryson, described as a colonial administrator, wired to KL for reinforcements. They duly arrived, but not before a group of rebels had seized a district office and burned the Union Jack. Bryson described the insurgents as 'the most aggressive Malays I have ever met. They were dressed for war; their heads were tightly bound with cloths; in their short sarongs – so short as to be almost like belts – were *parang panjang,* the vicious long knives.'

In real terms, these were minor incidents. But the fact that they occurred at all – peasants taking on the greatest military power in the world – belies the claim that British rule had wide support. The British experience might have been different had the mass of Malays not been so acquiescent – the result, no doubt, of a time when rajahs ruled ruthlessly and to demur at all could cost a man his life. 'The people had no initiative whatever,' wrote Frank Swettenham, known as 'the father and founder of modern Malaya': 'They were there to do the will of the Rajah or Chief under whose authority they lived.'

The richest of Malaya's rulers was also the most fiercely independent: Sultan Ibrahim of Johore. Ibrahim, who ruled from 1895 until 1959, a reign exceeding even Queen Victoria's, was slow to take direction. This created all sorts of problems for the British advisers, one of whom was our good friend Winstedt. But in 1932, the sultan met his match: a Scotswoman whom he made his wife and who, in turn, made him miserable.

The marriage lasted but a few years and then the sultan married again. His bride this time was Marcella Mendl, a twenty-five-year-old Romanian whom he met in London's Grosvenor House, where he had a suite, in October 1940 during an air raid. The sultan, as impetuous as ever, proposed on the spot, and the couple married two weeks later in Caxton Register Office.

Interviewed before the wedding, the sultan refused to discuss his previous marriage. 'I prefer to forget the past,' he said. 'It is for the future that I want to live. I fell in love directly I met Miss Mendl. We are going to be very happy.' Miss Mendl, described as highly educated and able to speak five languages, shared his optimism. A day after meeting the sultan, she said, she had introduced him to her mother, and the three had got along so well, they had had dinner together every night since. She also intimated – and one wonders if the sultan was aware of this – that she had invited Mother to live with them in Johore. One hopes the *ménage* proved a great success.

14

Against the Grain

Not every Briton in Malaya was a scoundrel. For every Ethel Proudlock, there was a Tristram Speedy, and for every E. N. T. Cummins, a Hubert Berkeley.

Speedy was born to adventure. He collected ivory in Sudan, fought the Maoris in New Zealand, and trained an army for the King of Abyssinia. All this before he was thirty. In 1874, he fetched up in Perak where, as an assistant resident, he acted briefly as town planner, laying out both Taiping and much of Kamunting. Something of a sybarite, he spent money freely, building himself an elaborate house and keeping a stable. A tall man with an impressive beard, he cut quite a dash. He loved to startle, often parading through Taiping wearing a leopard skin and turban, and playing 'The Campbells are Coming' on his bagpipes. When that ceased to shock, he took to riding an elephant. Speedy boasted of being a linguist, a claim some people disputed. No one, though, denied he had charm. He was also something of a tailor and was often to be seen hunched over a sewing machine. Much admired, he left Malaya in 1877.

Berkeley, an official known variously as the Last White Rajah and the Uncrowned King of Upper Perak, ruled his district as imperiously as any eastern potentate. He raised otters, toured his realm on an elephant – it was, he said, more comfortable than riding a horse – and thought so little of his superiors that he dispatched their letters to his outhouse without so much as opening them. His greatest eccentricity he reserved for the bench. On one occasion, unable to render a verdict in a case that turned on two opposing claims, this unorthodox magistrate, inspired perhaps by Solomon, ordered the litigants to engage in a tug-of-war, the victor in *that* contest winning the legal battle as well.

People like Speedy and Berkeley were relatively rare. They *liked* Malaya. The majority of Britons clearly did not. Some of these people have left us memoirs, most of which make for deadly reading. Some are earnest; some are brave; some strive to sound heroic; some evoke a sense of exile so keen it hurts to read them. And then there are the screeds, altogether far too many, decrying everything about the country: its awful climate, its awful jungle, its awful monotony, its awful natives. The only really interesting memoirs were penned by non-conformists: people like Winstedt and Lockhart and Bilainkin, men who, though lacking Speedy's daring and Berkeley's verve, were none the less their spiritual heirs – people whose response to Malaya was a deep one and whose contact with the country changed them for ever.

As much as they could, all three men steered clear of their more conventional compatriots. They seem, indeed, to have disliked them heartily. (Though not nearly as heartily as their compatriots disliked them.) Bilainkin preferred the company of Asians, he said, because they were spontaneous and 'mattered so much more to my real self than the twit-terings of persons who offer one a greeting of courtesy, weigh their words and calculate the effects of their expressions'.

Bilainkin was precocious. At seventeen he was writing leading articles for the *Nottingham Journal* and was only twenty-five when asked to edit Penang's *Straits Echo.* The job was a difficult one. His six predecessors had each lasted an average of five months, their letters of resignation citing deadline pressures and work days that began at 8 a.m. and all too often finished at midnight. But Bilainkin did not hesitate. This was his big chance; an opportunity, as he put it, to take on 'the race-consciousness maniacs'.

Bilainkin campaigned hard for racial tolerance. The term 'China man' was dropped from the *Echo*'s pages and replaced by the more neutral 'Chinese', and his editorials attacked everything from the practice of snapping fingers to summon a bar boy, to the way the British comported themselves in cinemas. Most of these attacks were well-reasoned, but once in a while his judgement failed him, and he became intolerant himself. Describing some mems at a dance he attended, he said, their dresses 'betrayed a greater acquaintance with the pattern for a taffeta or voile frock in a booklet given away with a twopenny weekly newspaper than with the dressmaker's fashion guide. If I had shut my eyes and opened them again, I should have concluded that I was at a mixed dance in a small village hall, where the tradesmen's daughters had arrived in their best finery bought in a neighbouring city store.'

Such occasional lapses aside, Bilainkin was a decent man who enjoyed a laugh. Shortly after arriving in Penang, he was visited in his office by a delegation of Indians. It had come to their attention, the Indians said gravely, that one of their number – an unscrupulous wizard – had cast a spell on the editor which put him in mortal danger. Bilainkin made a show of looking shocked and then, with equal gravity, assured the

Indians that the unscrupulous wizard would feel his wrath.

What offended Bilainkin more than anything was British arrogance. Britons refused to be interviewed by Asian reporters; refused to go parties if there were Asians present; refused to work for Asians whose qualifications exceeded their own; objected to addressing Asian magistrates as 'your worship'; demanded private rooms when they ate in Asian restaurants; and would rather die than consult an Asian doctor.

The worst offenders, said Bilainkin, were 'hooligans' and '*arrivistes*' – the first, former shop assistants who, in England, would have earned 'three pounds a week at thirty'; the second, 'men who have risen from humble positions and have not been to one of the public schools'. But at one time or another, everyone offended. The British behaved as if they owned Malaya, swaggering about like company directors at an annual general meeting.

As on all boards, the members of this one varied. There were men of distinction and men of vision; men of purpose and men of talent. Most were time-servers, though, Bilainkin said; people who had risen through the ranks, not because they were gifted, but because they had endured. British Malaya did not reward skill; it rewarded doggedness. It simply didn't do to be overly smart. Men like that were thought to be mercurial and ostentatious. They made people feel uncomfortable. It was the mediocre who got ahead.

Bilainkin often accused the British of forgetting their mission. They had come to Malaya claiming to be trustees, he said, and instead were running the country as if it were a colony. Malaya was not British property. It was (to use an analogy) a ward of court, and one day would want to control its own affairs. But how could it? Britain *spoke* of creating a Malay elite capable of ruling, but so far no much elite had emerged. Why? Because though they professed to like Malays, the British were sceptical of their abilities, sharing the view of the official in Calcutta who, asked to explain why the government of India did not include a single Indian, said he knew not a single Indian who was up to the job.

It was sheer chance that brought Winstedt to Malaya. He had wanted to serve in India and would have, too, if, taking the civil service exam, he had not misread an essay subject. Offered a job in either the FMS or the Straits Settlements, he chose the former because he thought its postage stamps more attractive. Before leaving England, he sought out an old Malaya hand. He wanted his stay in the FMS to be successful, Winstedt explained; what advice could he give him? The sage thought for a moment. Buy leather luggage, old boy, he said finally; nothing else will survive the weather.

'When you tread the soil of a country and live beneath its skies,' says a Malay proverb, 'follow the customs of that country.' Winstedt did precisely that. His compatriots were culture-bound; he was open. They, as much as they could, ignored Malaya; he embraced it. They associated only with one another; most of his friends were Malays. 'Like Gauguin,' he said, 'I have always wanted the urge of the unfamiliar to rouse me . . . I, therefore, turned eagerly to the Malays, who had, and still have for me, all the glamour of sportsmen, aristocrats and cynics.'

He also admired Malays for their excellent manners – by comparison, the British were boors – and their good looks: 'large dark eyes, sensuous lips well-cut . . . and a pale coffee-brown complexion.' The British, who never failed to remind him of forked radishes, were not in the same league at all. One Englishman of his acquaintance – and he may have been typical – was 'hairy of chest, rubicund of face, choleric of temper and perspiring even through the seat of his khaki shorts'. (Malays also thought the average Briton unprepossessing.

He looked, they said, like a boiled prawn and smelled like a fox.)

It galled Winstedt that most Britons in Malaya – though they wore solar topees and resided not far from the equator – lived lives that, for glamour, were every bit as pedestrian as the ones they had led in England. What they lacked, he said, was imagination. 'Romance', he tells us, 'depends less on scenery than on the temperament of the person viewing it', and then proceeds to provide an example. When, in 1902, Winstedt sailed to Malaya for the first time, his travelling companion was another civil service cadet who, when he saw Penang, turned away in disgust. What was the matter? asked Winstedt. Did he find the island less than beautiful? No. Not that. The cadet, 'worrying with anguished brow', had just made a dreadful discovery: the precious calling cards he had had printed at enormous expense had been left behind in England.

If Winstedt had calling cards, he cannot have used them very much. Calling was the least of his concerns. He had work to do. While in Malaya, he wrote – in his own time – the first Malay grammar, an English–Malay dictionary, and a history of Malay literature. The latter is hated by some Malays, by the way, offended by its claim that many of the forms they prize so much are not theirs at all, but were borrowed from other cultures. Much like Trollope, Winstedt rose at four in the morning and wrote until eight when he turned to what he called his *real* work – his duties as a civil servant.

Winstedt left Malaya in 1935 and for the rest of his life – he died in 1966 two months shy of his eighty-eighth birthday – pined for the place. He felt constrained in England. 'When I sit in the tube in the murk of a winter evening and see lonely boys and girls returning from the dull jobs that bolster the ugly civilization to which we cling so avidly and so prodigally,

I feel that I want to exchange Big Ben for Stonehenge and the sun.'

Lockhart was a colourful character, too. Born in Scotland in 1887, he learned while young, he tells us, not only to respect *all* cultures, but also the secret of mastering foreign languages (which, sadly, he does not divulge). Some of his schooling he received in Paris where his tutor was Paul Passy, a Calvinist who ate rats, believing it would increase his mettle. For a time, Lockhart wrote short stories 'with morbid settings and unhappy endings' in the style of Pierre Loti whom he would later meet. 'His eccentricities and mincing manners failed to cure me of an admiration which I feel to this day for the charm and beauty of his prose.'

Lockhart may have inspired Maugham's story 'P. & O.' in which Mr Gallagher, a rubber planter, leaves his Malay lover, intending to return to Ireland. But without his knowledge, the woman has put a spell on him and, halfway between Bombay and Aden, he falls ill and dies. Lockhart was also a planter, also had a Malay lover whom he abandoned, and also fell terribly ill. The voyage back to England was a nightmare, he writes in *Memoirs of a British Agent*: 'I wanted to die . . .'

He recovered, however, and, in 1911, joined the Foreign Office where, when not playing football in the corridors, he watched elderly clerks with quill pens and ink pots copying reports. (Civil servants were like the fountains in Trafalgar Square, he was told. They played from ten to four.) Later, he was posted to Moscow where, in 1917, he was imprisoned by the communists on charges that he, along with several others, had conspired to murder Trotsky and Lenin, blow up railway bridges and overthrow the government. Lockhart denied all involvement and would later return to London and a job at the *Evening Standard*.

Lockhart was another who loved Malaya, even professing to

like its heat. 'The glowing warmth of the tropical sun', he said, 'became a necessity of my physical existence and a stimulant to my mind.' Like the hero of Henri Fauconnier's novel *The Soul of Malaya*, he came to believe 'that every country where a man cannot live naked in all seasons is condemned to work, to war, and to the hampering restraint of moral codes. Today, the fogs of an English winter are to me as grim a nightmare as the walls of my Bolshevik prison.'

Fauconnier, a Frenchman living in Selangor when Mrs Proudlock resided there, was part rubber planter, part mystic. His novel, about the search for transcendence, was published in 1908 and, needless to say, was to prove controversial. Its detractors dismissed it as metaphysical nonsense, a work so naive it could appeal only to arrant sentimentalists and aesthetes – a term which, in the wake of the Oscar Wilde trials, conjured up all sorts of unpleasantness.

For those who had tired of Malaya's crassness and vulgarity, though, the book became a rallying point. One fan, writing in the *Mail* in 1911, said civilization had divorced man from nature to the extent that the Malay peasant living in his kampong knew more about the world than the person who had been to Eton or Marlborough. 'An environment of natives of all colours and creeds is a better school of life than your mullioned common room.'

This was strong stuff, and the writer, very sensibly, did not append his name. It was well known in Malaya that, unless you were brilliant (like Winstedt) or lived in slightly-more-liberal Penang (like Bilainkin), dissenters got short shrift. William Proudlock's is the classic case, but there were others, too; people who, though their punishment may not have been as harsh, paid dearly for speaking their minds.

The man who preceded Bilainkin as editor of the *Straits Echo* was Richard Sidney, who turned to journalism after leaving VI in 1926. As an educator – one thinks of all that Housman – Sidney had his shortcomings. But VI prospered during his tenure, and his students revered him. What did him in was his failure to hobnob. Shy by nature and disliking drink, he avoided the Spotted Dog, and this offended people. He was aloof, they complained. 'Aloof' meant that you thought yourself better than others and this always rankled, not because KL was fiercely egalitarian – clearly it wasn't that – but because it was just within the realm of possibility that you *were* better.

At a time when the attitudes of the races had polarized, Sidney kept company with Chinese and Malays, going to the theatre with them and taking them on motoring tours. Even worse: he gave every impression of enjoying himself, which compromised him further. One wasn't supposed to enjoy Malaya. Malaya was something to be endured, counting the days until the tour expired. Sidney's behaviour flew in the face of convention, and the British watched, their resentment mounting.

Retribution was exacted in 1926 when Sidney was fired. The official explanation was that he and the government disagreed, but since the dispute involved nothing more serious than Sidney's pressing the Education Department to undertake some long overdue school repairs, the firing is more likely to have been punitive.

His dismissal seems to have unnerved him. His tenure at the *Straits Echo* was short-lived, paper and editor parting company, Bilainkin tells us, after just six months on terms that were 'mutually agreed'. For a time, Sidney returned to England, but was back in Malaya when Japan invaded and spent the rest of the war in a concentration camp where, to boost morale, he gave a series of lectures. (He was something of an expert on Arnold Bennett.) In his later years, he fell on hard times and died in 1966 'a lonely man'.

If the period between 1880 and 1896, when the FMS came into being, was dominated by the pioneers, the years between 1900 and 1920 were a time of consolidation. Malaya was more conventional now, and not everyone was happy about it. The British had become a lot of sheep, one man claimed in 1911: 'I belong to a generation which neither thinks, sees, or hears for itself.' Others complained that Malaya no longer *felt* like Malaya. It had been domesticated, and where once tigers had roamed, now there were tennis courts and cricket creases.

'Thirty odd years ago, we had no cold storage in Kuala Lumpur, no electric light, no water laid on, no motor cars, no cinemas . . . no weekly dances,' the *Mail* said in 1922. 'But thank goodness we did not feel as if we were living in a London suburb.'

In the old days, life, while less comfortable, was a lot more exciting, said the *Mail*, waxing nostalgic. People used to enjoy themselves. Once, 'a respected citizen attending a merry party on a boat . . . let himself down the wind shaft into the saloon where the ladies were resting in *déshabillée*. What a reception he got!' On another occasion, two women crawled under the Selangor Club – the building back then was raised on piles – to eavesdrop on a smoking concert which, by tradition, women were barred from attending. 'They were ultimately discovered (given away by their laughter) and taken into the bar and treated to refreshment.'

Progress had come at a price, and the *Mail* wondered if the game had been worth the candle. Were people any happier for having telephones? Quite the opposite, it said. People did not entertain as much as they once had, and they were not as friendly. They had become guarded, weighing everything they did, everything they said, terrified lest they compromise themselves. And their goals had changed. All anyone thought about now was money. Commerce had once been a sedate affair. To survive now, a businessman had to be ruthless. In the past, people made money. Lots of it, in some cases. Yet mixed in with all that entrepreneurial zeal was an element of altruism. They were not just serving *their* interests; they were serving Malaya's as well. That spirit no longer existed, said the *Mail.* People cared nothing about Malaya. It didn't matter to them where they lived. In Malaya, in Nigeria, in the Transvaal, it was all the same – as long as they were getting rich.

A few brave souls even complained that British policy had erred. It was a mistake, they said, to have placed such emphasis on material progress, a mistake to fill the country with people who never wondered if, instead of Malays adopting British values, more might have been achieved had the British adopted theirs. Echoing the man who rejected 'the mullioned common room' two decades earlier, a member of the FMS legislature caused an uproar in 1933 when he suggested that the British had as much to learn from 'Malay civilization as we trustees have to give of our own. And if we bring to them the best we have – our science and the alleviation of sickness – and leave them their own traditions and mode of life instead of the false values of our western materialism, Malaya and indeed the world would be the better for it.'

By then it was much too late. The Japanese occupation was a mere eight years away. But eight years or eighty, it hardly mattered because these people had long lost the capacity to change. Their sense of what had been sacrificed to come here had become a psychosis that blinded them to all that had been gained. Peet recognized this, telling his fellow expatriates that, as long as they craved England, happiness would always elude them. 'I fear that you, like most of us, would have to admit that your most peaceful moments have been marred in Malaya by a faint, but deep unrest,' he wrote. 'You are paying the penalty of exile and unless you give up home leave, unless you cease to dream about retirement in a white man's country, and unless you so attach yourself to Malaya that this country means to you what England used to mean, you can never hope to know beneath the tropic stars the unimaginable peace of an English summer night.'

The British ignored him. Though many would end up spending most of their adult lives in Malaya, they never thought of themselves as anything but sojourners, their devotion to England so fierce it left them deranged. If only they had been more sensible, if only they had tried harder, but they chose, instead, to languish, counting off the days and longing for release like boys in a boarding school pining for the start of summer.

They suffered terribly for their obduracy. Does this explain their awful behaviour? Between 1900 and 1940, the heyday of British rule, the British in the FMS produced one scandal after another, a record all the more remarkable when you consider the size of the community: at their most numerous, there were never more than 6,000 of them.

People died violently, and their deaths were put down to accidents; women were molested; servants were assaulted; labourers were beaten; and while it might be argued that these were egregious acts, the work of a small minority, there is no doubt at all they were widely condoned. Even eighty years ago, this is not how decent people were supposed to behave.

Asians were not the only ones the British mistreated. Most Britons in Malaya were drawn from the same echelons of the middle class and had attended the same public schools. The exceptions were the train drivers. In 1926, there were fifty of them and, because they were working-class, they were barred from British clubs and discouraged from attending British sporting events. Their wives got short shrift, too. Those who ventured into John Little's Tea Room, popular with the wives of civil servants, were treated so peremptorily that few of them ventured back.

Because they earned so little, the drivers, to make a living, were forced to work eighteen-hour days. Several, in fact, worked themselves to death, but there was widespread opposition to raising their pay. Doing so would be a mistake, the *Times of Malaya* argued. Given more money, the drivers would spend it on drink and act like a lot of louts.

Did the British have reason to be this high-handed? They certainly thought so. The train drivers were seen as threatening their prestige which, if impaired, would compromise their ability to rule. And that rule, they believed, had accomplished much. 'Ours is a record of great achievement by courageous and masterful men,' one official wrote. But examine that record and the achievement begins to look ambiguous. According to the government, it had given Malaya much: roads and railways, a legal system, an efficient administration, and a booming economy. Yet much of this was financed, not with public monies, but by private investment, some of it from Malaya's Chinese, some from overseas. Westminster made it clear from the outset that no help would be forthcoming from the British Treasury; if Malaya was to be developed, it would have to find the funds itself. When the economy *did* boom, relatively few Asians reaped the spoils. The real beneficiaries were international investors with stock in the tin mines and rubber estates, and the expatriates themselves who lived like princes.

Maugham never much liked the British in Malaya. Interviewed by the *Mail* when he visited KL in 1925, he described them as churlish; people who, while enjoying every convenience civilization had to offer, did nothing but grumble about 'the hardships of exile'.

('The first thing that strikes one about Mr. Maugham', said

the *Mail*'s reporter, 'is his piercing black eyes which seem never to cease observing even when their owner is talking and thinking of matters far removed from his surroundings.')

The Briton in Malaya, Maugham claimed in his short stories, was 'never part of the life about him . . . He is a pale stranger who moves through all this reality like a being from another planet.' Bored with themselves and with one another, the British went to pot.

They became slothful. ('It was lovely to have nothing to do from morning till night, except play the gramophone, or patience, and read novels.')

They took to drink. ('He used to go to bed every night with a bottle of whisky and empty it before morning.')

They aged before their time. ('One's an elderly man at fifty, and at fifty-five one is good for nothing but the scrap-heap.')

They grew unkempt. ('I never met a woman who obviously cared so little about the way she looked.')

They went to seed. ('I don't suppose he read a book from year's end to year's end.')

Malaya was furious, the *Straits Times* accusing Maugham of focusing exclusively on 'the worst and least representative aspects of European life in Malaya – murder, cowardice, drink, seduction, adultery . . . always the same cynical emphasis on the same unpleasant things'.

Maugham claimed to be surprised by the uproar and, stung by charges that he had maligned an entire community, sought to make amends. 'The reader must not suppose that the incidents I have narrated are of common occurrence,' he wrote in a preface to his *Collected Short Stories.* 'The vast majority of these people, government servants, planters and traders, who spent their working lives in Malaya were ordinary people ordinarily satisfied with their station in life . . . They were good, decent, normal.'

Given what we know about Maugham's rather grim *Weltanschauung*, words like 'normal' and 'ordinary' hardly constitute a ringing endorsement. But, as the preceding pages make clear, it was not simply Maugham who maligned the British; the British did quite enough of that themselves.

'The tendency out here', the *Mail* said, 'is for everyone to live exactly after the style of the well-to-do; to keep up the same table equipment, to follow the same pursuits, to become in fact dumb treaders of the same social mill.' How exhausting it must have been, this pressure to look and act and sound and think like everyone else. And what resentment it must have bred: the constant snooping, the nosing round. In time, one's countrymen must have come to seem like gaolers.

III

Home

15

The Vanishing

Maugham's play *The Letter*, adapted from his short story, opened at the Playhouse in London's West End on 24 February 1927 with Gladys Cooper in the role of Leslie Crosbie. The set – a planter's bungalow boasting rattan furniture, sun hats, blow pipes and a mounted tiger's head – was praised for its realism and was, according to Maugham, 'a faithful copy from a photograph I brought back from my last voyage to that part of the world'.

The one incongruity was a gold embroidered coat, purchased by Maugham in a KL pawnshop, worn by the Chinese mistress. A person of her class could never have afforded such a garment, said a woman writing in the *Malay Mail* nine months later. People like her 'always wore . . . a white baju and black trousers'. When the inconsistency was brought to Maugham's attention, he said that, having carted the coat all the way from Malaya, 'it might as well appear in the play'. *The Letter* ran for 338 performances.

Under the headline, 'KL Tragedy Recalled', the *Malay Mail* reviewed *The Letter* on 31 March, remarking that Maugham had 'followed pretty closely the lines of a *cause célèbre* which actually occurred here in Selangor 15 or 16 years ago, though whether he has provided the correct solution of the accused woman's motive for shooting her victim is still a matter of conjecture'.

KL had been braced for *The Letter* ever since November 1925 when Maugham, visiting the capital of the FMS for a second time, told the *Mail* in a brief interview at Carcosa that he was adapting a short story of his which had been 'suggested by a tragedy some of the actors in which are in KL today'. Maugham stressed the word 'suggested'. Yes, he had heard of the Proudlock case four years earlier, 'but in the course of writing, incidents and characters change until the original is almost lost sight of'.

One month after *The Letter* opened, a man writing in the *Mail* said he had reason to believe that Mr and Mrs Proudlock were still alive. There is no reason why they would not have been, of course; in 1927, they would still have been comparatively young. This, though, was not the writer's point. He was expressing his concern that the play – were they to see it or hear of its existence – might cause them some distress.'It may be, of course, that Mr Maugham ascertained that this was not the case before he dished this ghastly tragedy as a work of imagination,' the writer goes on. Even so, he said, it might have been better if Maugham had resisted the impulse to write the play at all and left its 'sordid subject in the oblivion where it so long reposed'.

It's possible that Ethel and William Proudlock *did* hear about *The Letter,* though it is unlikely that either of them saw it. In 1927, the evidence suggests, the Proudlocks had for some time been living overseas. Shortly after returning from Malaya in 1911, the two, along with their young daughter, seem to have disappeared.

Arriving in London in December 1911, Proudlock went to ground briefly and then, early in 1912, remembering perhaps that Saturday afternoon in Klang when, flat on his back, he collected his wits and scored that most unlikely goal, he took aim once again. This time, his target was nothing less than the British government.

Over the next several months, Proudlock became the bane of the Colonial Office. Writing to the Secretary of State, he demanded redress both for himself, in the shape of a new appointment, and for his wife who, he continued to insist, had been horribly wronged. When that did not work, he had others write on his behalf. He petitioned members of parliament – one of them was Ramsay MacDonald – and, with the help of a friend, gained the attention (though not for long) of a member of the House of Lords. Proudlock wanted justice. He had, he felt, been duped, and his sense of fairness demanded satisfaction. In the beginning, he seems to have thought that the injury done him had originated in Malaya and would be righted by alerting the authorities in London. But time disabused him of that notion as, little by little, it was brought home to him that redress would not be forthcoming. The Colonial Office had no intention of righting any wrongs for the reason that some of those wrongs had been done, not just with London's knowledge, but at its instigation.

In February 1912, Proudlock wrote to the Colonial Office for what would be the last time. The letter, written from an address in Bromley, Kent, is eleven pages long and marked private and confidential. That he was growing desperate is evident, not just from his tone, but also from the fact that he acted out of character: William Proudlock issued a threat.

'If any of my remarks should strike you as wanting in tact,' he told Lewis Harcourt, Secretary of State for the Colonies, 'I ask you to place yourself for one moment in my unenviable position and also to remember that they have at least the virtue of being honest.'

Describing his ten years in KL as the happiest of his life, Proudlock for the first time named names: Sir Arthur Young, whom he accused of orchestrating the effort to force him out of his job; and J. O. Anthonisz and Edward Broadrick, both of whom gave him to understand that work would be found for him elsewhere. Without these assurances, he added, he would never have agreed to leave.

Turning now to the subject of the murder trial, he said the assessors 'were prejudiced by the filthy lies that were afloat concerning my wife and me – stories that I have every reason to believe emanated from the police'. The latter, he went on, 'were very vindictive and did everything in their power to show that improper relations had existed between my wife and the deceased man, Mr Steward. I can assure you that directly I heard the story I thoroughly satisfied myself that there was no truth in it.'

Finishing, Proudlock described himself as the victim of a grave injustice as a consequence of which he was prevented from pursuing a career in the East. Why was he being punished like this? Because, he said, in an effort to clear his name, he had exposed 'the disgraceful state of things in police administration [in the FMS] – an exposure which I believe has been smoothed over in a disgraceful way.'

Then he issued his warning. The editor of London's *Daily Mail* had shown an interest in his story and 'is most anxious to have full particulars for publication'. Proudlock said he was loath to enlist the press. It was justice he sought; not notoriety. And besides, he wished to spare the feelings, not only of his wife, but of Steward's family as well. For that reason he was asking the Colonial Secretary one last time to procure him a job similar to the one he had held at VI and to pay him the sum of $1,300 – 'the full amount that I am out of pocket by the libel action being decided against me'.

The letter ended: 'I *think* I have the honour to be, sir, yours obediently, W. Proudlock.' (My italics.)

As moving as the letter is, it touched no hearts in Whitehall. The Colonial Office had Proudlock where it wanted him. It had forced a man who for months had had to endure official deceit to do something which would simply have confirmed its suspicions about him. The demand for payment is 'perhaps characteristic of Mr. Proudlock', a civil servant wrote on a note attached to his letter. He went on: 'the last paragraph is blackmail pure and simple . . . Reply that the Secretary of State is not able to interfere with judicial proceedings and that he [Proudlock] has no prospect, as has already been stated [of being offered further employment].'

Proudlock never did make good his threat – in all likelihood he never meant to – and in March 1912, he and his wife left Kent to stay with A. H. Barlow, then living in Leighton, Bedfordshire. It was from Leighton, on 3 April, that Barlow wrote to Cecil Harmsworth, his representative in parliament, asking him to intervene on the Proudlocks' behalf. In his letter, Barlow described Will and Ethel as 'intimate friends' whom he had known for ten years and with whom he had once lived in the FMS.

Proudlock, he said, was 'indignant beyond measure at the abominable methods of the officials and the gross perjury that had taken place'. Barlow also indicated that he had discussed the case with a member of the House of Lords who 'is prepared to ask a question in parliament on being provided with sufficient material to warrant his taking such a course'. He finished with this endorsement: 'Personally, I vouch for the absolute integrity and transparent honesty of Mr and Mrs Proudlock.'

Though Harmsworth forwarded this letter to the Colonial Office for comment, nothing came of it.

William Proudlock never did find the justice he sought. There was no redress for him; no exoneration for his wife. But what must have weighed most heavily on him through all of this was the realization that the people he had most admired, the people he had tried so hard and for so long to emulate, were nothing but hypocrites. When he fell from favour, not one of them defended him. He had become a pariah and rather than risk their own chances, people avoided him.

And what became of Ethel? There were rumours that, shortly after reaching England, she had a nervous breakdown. This may be true. When writing to his MP, Barlow had enclosed a photograph of her (it was later destroyed) in which, according to an official who saw it, she looked ghastly. What was not true was the rumour that she died in a lunatic asylum. Ethel didn't die in England. None of the Proudlocks did. After being driven from Malaya, they found England to be no more welcoming and pulled up stakes again, this time to live in Canada.

In June 1913, Will and Ethel boarded the *Royal Edward* for Quebec. Dorothy remained with a relative in England – presumably to give her parents a chance to establish themselves – and wouldn't join her mother and father until the following year. The Proudlocks settled in Portage la Prairie in Manitoba, chosen, one might guess, for its remoteness.

Then, in August 1916, Ethel, without her husband and without her daughter, moved to the United States, crossing the border at St. Albans in Vermont. She told U.S. immigration officials that she was headed for Sioux Falls, South Dakota (a lie, it turned out; her destination was New York City), and when asked if she had ever been in prison – it was one of the questions on the form she was given – she replied that she had not. Under the heading 'Calling' or 'Occupation', she wrote the single word 'attendant'. The official who interviewed her that day adjudged her to be in good health, noted that she had in her possession a total of $80 – $30 more than the required legal minimum – and, after estimating her height at just over five feet, told her she could now enter the United States.

Seven years later, Dorothy, who had remained in Portage la Prairie, also moved to the U.S., joining her mother in Brooklyn.

In her book *Hard Scrabble*, published privately in the 1960s, Mabel Marsh speculated that her former kindergarten teacher 'ended her days in New York City'. But this was not the case. In 1950, Ethel and Dorothy moved to Florida.

What Ethel did in New York is something of a mystery, but this is understandable. She had every reason to avoid the public eye. Her situation was a sensitive one, after all. Were it ever discovered that she was a killer, she might well have been deported. The Florida years are easier to reconstruct because there Ethel lived more openly. She was now a naturalized U.S. citizen which, no doubt, gave her confidence. For the first time in her life, she belonged somewhere.

Dorothy married when she was eighteen – the marriage was not a success – and wed again in 1944. Her second husband was Gerald Arnett, and it was he who suggested the move to Florida. After a long career in the U.S. military, Gerald retired in 1949 and, a year later, was working as a security guard for a Miami bank. In 1953, the Arnetts bought a house – curiously, it was registered in Dorothy's name – in a Miami neighborhood known as Sunkist Grove. Ethel, now in her sixties, rented a nearby apartment where she lived alone. According to one of Dorothy's in-laws, Ethel's garden had a swing in which she would sit sometimes and talk about her dead husband.

For part of this period, however, Will wasn't dead. In 1930 he was back in England and looking for a job. In January of the following year he found one – a teaching post at St George's College, a private boys' school in Buenos Aires. He joined his new school a few months later, eventually becoming joint headmaster. He was never to leave Argentina. He retired from St George's in 1953 and died in Buenos Aires four years later at the age of seventy-seven. The cause of death was attributed to heart failure.

During his tenure at St George's it was school policy to employ only single teachers, and for that reason Will represented himself as a bachelor. In fact, he stayed in touch with his wife and child and, up until the time he died, regularly sent them money. To preserve the 'single man' fiction, Dorothy, when she wrote to him, began her letters, 'Dear Uncle Will . . .'

I admire William Proudlock. His strength and goodness, his loyalty and the love he bore his wife have about them something noble. He is the hero of this sad, unpleasant story. He alone emerges with his honour intact.

The Arnetts' home, the house in which Ethel would breathe her last, looked dilapidated when I saw it in September 1998. Cramped and sad and set in an ugly garden, it looked so mean, my heart sank. This was a far cry from the bungalow in Malaya. The two houses, though, have this in common: both have verandahs, and both have been the scenes of shootings. In June 1998, the current owner (Dorothy sold the house in 1986) narrowly escaped being killed when a burglar climbed through a window and shot him while he slept. The incident so unnerved the man, the house is now abandoned.

In the 1950s, both Ethel and Dorothy were gainfully employed, Ethel as a nurse in a doctor's office and Dorothy as a bookkeeper for the Copeland Pipe and Supply Co. One of Dorothy's co-workers and a good friend at Copeland's described her to me as tall and blonde and fun to be around. Dorothy was something of an entertainer who, when living in New York, had done some theatre work, none of it of any great importance. She abandoned the stage when she moved to Florida.

Ethel, true to form, seems to have kept much to herself in Miami, but one Christmas she surprised Dorothy's colleague by turning up at Copeland's with a present for her, a brightly coloured, patchwork shawl she had crocheted herself. Ethel, the colleague said, struck her as 'very sweet' and much like Dorothy in appearance. The two, she added, 'were very close'. Though not so close, I suspect, that Dorothy knew much of Ethel's past. Dorothy, I am guessing, had no inkling at all that her mother had been tried for murder.

Ethel died on 22 September 1974 at the age of eighty-eight. (Her death certificate lists her date of birth as 1886 which, if correct, would make her twenty five when she killed William Steward; not twenty-three, as she claimed.) Death was caused by cardiac arrest. Five years earlier, Ethel had been diagnosed as having arteriosclerotic heart disease complicated by chronic bronchitis and emphysema. Her remains were cremated. Three months later, Dorothy suffered a second loss. On 31 December, her husband died of a heart attack while mowing the lawn.

Dorothy survived both of them by sixteen years, dying on 12 January 1990. She was eighty-three. In 1985, she succumbed to dementia and was named a ward of court. Her legal guardian, a Miami lawyer, remembers her as a cheerful woman who loved crossword puzzles and had a house full of cats. It was also her practice to feed the neighborhood pigeons, which made her unpopular with Sunkist Grove's other residents. Dorothy spent the last five years of her life in a retirement home. Like her mother, she was cremated. Though she died childless, she liked children and often volunteered at a local elementary school.

One of the great puzzles about Steward's death is why the authorities, who must have known the harm it would inflict on British prestige, allowed the case to go to trial. I feel I can answer that question now. What did for Mrs Proudlock was not the murder or her infidelity, both of which, had it suited those in power, could have been kept quiet. What sealed her fate was that, in addition to being a killer and an adulteress, she was also almost certainly Eurasian.

Eurasians, who were never more than tolerated in Malaya, had, by 1911, become objects of scorn. (And Mrs Proudlock did nothing to raise their stock. It is worth noting that, one month after the murder, a Eurasian woman, for the first time ever, was prevented from entering Raffles ballroom.) Eurasians were accused of embodying the worst features of *both* races and were said to be feckless, lacking in loyalty and unreliable. 'Eurasians visiting Europe', said Bilainkin, a man whose sympathies were usually generous, 'claim in the presence of untravelled Europeans that they are "white". They can be detected easily by the inferiority complex which they cannot suppress and by a tendency, in the absence in the company of other Eurasians, to despise the products of mixed unions.'

Maugham, who has been accused of stirring up anti-Eurasian sentiment, seems to have disliked them as much as anyone. Izzart, in his story 'Yellow Streak', is painfully conscious that he has 'a touch of the tar-brush' and compensates by talking about his regiment all the time and making far too much of having been to Harrow. He hates his thin legs – they looked like a Malay's – and, as Ethel must have, wonders what his English colleagues would think if they knew he had native blood: 'They wouldn't say he was gay and friendly then, they would say he was damned familiar, and they would say he was inefficient and careless, as the half-castes were, and when he talked of marrying a white woman, they would snigger ... Every one knew that you couldn't rely on Eurasians, sooner or later they would let you down.'

In Maugham's play *East of Suez*, two men discuss Freddy Baker who has just married a Eurasian. 'It can't be very nice', says one, 'to have a wife whom even the missionary ladies turn up their noses at.' 'He'll never get a good job with a Eurasian wife,' says the other. 'Freddy Baker will be sent to two-penny halfpenny outposts where his wife doesn't matter.' The Eurasian, he adds, is vulgar and noisy and couldn't tell the truth if he tried. 'He's crooked from the crown of his German hat to the toes of his American boots.'

It was not until *after* he married that Proudlock heard of his wife's questionable parentage. In 1908, the day had long gone when a 'respectable' man – if he wished to remain so – married a Eurasian. Why did no one tell him? Ethel would not have done so, of course, and neither would the Charters. This was their chance to get her off their hands.

They were strivers, Will and Ethel. Each had something to prove, something to live down: he his working-class background and she the circumstances of her birth. Who knows? Had KL been just a bit more tolerant, they might have succeeded. It was not a kind place. In 1911, in the wake of the decision to exclude Asians from the civil service and the attempt to segregate the trains, more and more emphasis was being placed on racial purity. Bloodlines mattered now, and Mrs Proudlock, as much as she tried to ape the mems, found herself increasingly excluded.

Appearances in Ethel's case proved misleading. While she

looked shy and retiring, a quiet woman who adored her daughter and doted on her husband, she was quite the opposite. She seethed with dissatisfaction. She resented her poor state of health; she resented the ambiguity surrounding her birth; she resented her socially ambitious husband whose efforts to get ahead meant he was rarely home; she resented the condescension of the mems, who would have made no secret of the fact that they considered her inferior. (That they consorted with her at all was largely on account of her popular father and well-intentioned husband; but for them, she would have been ostracized completely.)

Mrs Proudlock would never have been more than suffered in KL. Everyone knew her secret. She was an interloper. People did not treat her with the same cordiality they extended to others. With rare exceptions, they did not invite her to their homes. In KL, people gave dinner parties all the time; Ethel attended few of them. She seems to have been largely friendless. The Spotted Dog was famous for its cliques, most people belonging to one or more. Mrs Proudlock belonged to none at all. There must have been times when she felt horribly lonely. No wonder she spent so much of her time in bed.

Mrs Proudlock had many reasons to be resentful and all the time in the world to brood on them. When she emptied her revolver into Steward that night, she was not only punishing him for the indignity he had inflicted on her, she was avenging every indignity she had ever suffered: the unhappy marriage, the father who cared little for her, the stepmother who avoided her as much as she could, the contempt of those who should have been her peers. These – and all the other frustrations that women of her class and time and place were made to endure – are what made her pull the trigger. If Steward had not turned up that night, it was only a matter of time before Ethel Proudlock would train that gun on someone else – her father, perhaps, or even her husband.

Mrs Proudlock did not only end Steward's life and blight her husband's; another of her victims was her sister. On Saturday 4 November 1911, Marjorie Charter was to have married Edgar Wallace in St Mary's Church, KL. 'The ceremony was arranged to take place at half past one, but at that time the bridegroom had not arrived,' the *Mail* reported. 'The officiating minister, the Rev. P. G. Grahame, and guests were present at the church and, after waiting half an hour, left.'

Much of KL applauded Wallace's decision. Who in his right mind, people asked, would want as in-laws a murderer and a man whose criticism of the authorities had made him a pariah?

The murder also divided Steward's family. In March 1914, J. B. Steward, the dead man's older brother, wrote to 'The British Consul, Singapore', from Vernon, British Columbia, to ask if 'you could see your way to put my mind at rest a little'. What, he wanted to know, 'was the feeling . . . out there' about the murder?

The older Steward had been one of those who opposed hanging Ethel, giving as his reasons the fact that he, like her, had a daughter and because 'the only lips that could really have condemned the wretched woman were sealed. I do not envy her her life if she were guilty.' His attitude, he said, had caused a 'considerable rift' in his family, 'and the whole thing worries me not a little especially as I have since developed spinal trouble and have all my time to think'.

Steward, however, his generosity notwithstanding, received little satisfaction from the tight-lipped 'consul'. His letter, directed to the Resident in Selangor, elicited one of those infuriatingly non-committal official replies: 'Sir, I am directed . . . to inform you . . . that the Resident is not in a position to express an opinion on the matter.'

The Proudlock trial did not create anti-British feeling in Malaya. That had always existed. It did help, however, to augment and consolidate it. There had always been those who questioned Britain's right to rule. But until 1911, their numbers were small. Most of Malaya's population – rulers as well as ruled – believed the myths on which the British based their authority. Steward's death and its consequences made belief in these myths more difficult.

The British had damaged themselves in Asian eyes before, both when the colour bar in the civil service was instituted and when attempts were made to segregate the trains. Apologists could rationalize these earlier actions as wrong-headed or insensitive. But murder of one member of the ruling class by another, along with the controversy engendered by the trial which followed, severely weakened the British claims that they were morally superior. The myths had started looking threadbare. To an increasing number of Asians, it was apparent now that their rulers were not some master race come to civilize a backward country, but a people with force at their disposal out to line their pockets. The British had been demystified.

The political impact of this was slow to manifest itself, and decades would pass before an independence movement would emerge. But one immediate result was a growing cynicism on both sides of the racial divide. With no culture to speak of and little intellectual life, Malaya became first and last a mercantile society – vulgar, crass and materialistic – a first-rate place, the saying went, for second-rate people.

Index